D1304566

Presented To:

_____

From:

_____

Date:

_____

THE POWER
of the
ETERNAL
NOW

THE POWER

of the

ETERNAL

NOW

Living in the Realm of I AM

JEREMY LOPEZ

© Copyright 2011–Jeremy Lopez

All rights reserved. This book is protected by the copyright laws of the United States of America. This book may not be copied or reprinted for commercial gain or profit. The use of short quotations or occasional page copying for personal or group study is permitted and encouraged. Permission will be granted upon request. Unless otherwise identified, Scripture quotations are taken from the King James Version. Scripture quotations marked NASB are taken from the NEW AMERICAN STANDARD BIBLE®, Copyright © 1960, 1962, 1963, 1968, 1971, 1972, 1973, 1975, 1977, 1995 by The Lockman Foundation. Used by permission. Scripture quotations marked NIV are taken from the HOLY BIBLE, NEW INTERNATIONAL VERSION®, Copyright © 1973, 1978, 1984 Biblica. Used by permission of Zondervan. All rights reserved. Scripture quotations marked MSG are taken from The Message. Copyright © 1993, 1994, 1995, 1996, 2000, 2001, 2002. Used by permission of NavPress Publishing Group. Scripture quotations marked NKJV are taken from the New King James Version®. Copyright © 1982 by Thomas Nelson, Inc. Used by permission. All rights reserved. Scripture quotations marked RSV are taken from The Holy Bible: Revised Standard Version. Copyright 1946, 1952, 1959, 1973 by the Division of Christian Education of the National Council of the Churches of Christ in the United States of America. All rights reserved. Used by permission. Scripture quotations marked TNIV are taken from the HOLY BIBLE, TODAY'S NEW INTERNATIONAL VERSION® TNIV® Copyright © 2001, 2005 by Biblica®. All rights reserved worldwide. Scripture quotations marked NLT are taken from the Holy Bible, New Living Translation, copyright 1996, 2004. Used by permission of Tyndale House Publishers., Wheaton, Illinois 60189. All rights reserved. Scripture quotations marked JB are from The Jerusalem Bible, copyright © 1966 by Darton, Longman & Todd, Ltd. and Doubleday, a division of Bantam Doubleday Dell Publishing Group, Inc. Reprinted by permission. Scripture quotations marked NJB are from The New Jerusalem Bible, copyright © 1985 by Darton, Longman & Todd, Ltd. and Doubleday, a division of Random House, Inc. Reprinted by Permission. Emphasis within Scripture quotations is the author's own. Please note that Destiny Image's publishing style capitalizes certain pronouns in Scripture that refer to the Father, Son, and Holy Spirit, and may differ from some publishers' styles. Take note that the name satan and related names are not capitalized. We choose not to acknowledge him, even to the point of violating grammatical rules.

DESTINY IMAGE® PUBLISHERS, INC.

P.O. Box 310, Shippensburg, PA 17257-0310

"Speaking to the Purposes of God for This Generation and for the Generations to Come."

This book and all other Destiny Image, Revival Press, Mercy Place, Fresh Bread, Destiny Image Fiction, and Treasure House books are available at Christian bookstores and distributors worldwide.

For a U.S. bookstore nearest you, call 1-800-722-6774.

For more information on foreign distributors, call 717-532-3040.

Reach us on the Internet: www.destinyimage.com.

ISBN 13 TP: 978-0-7684-3824-6
ISBN 13 HC: 978-0-7684-3825-3
ISBN 13 LP: 978-0-7684-3826-0
ISBN 13 Ebook: 978-0-7684-8981-1

For Worldwide Distribution, Printed in the U.S.A.

1 2 3 4 5 6 7 8 9 10 11 / 13 12 11

Dedication

I dedicate this book to my parents, Jim and Jeanne Lopez, who never stop showing unconditional love toward me and all those who know them. Also, to my staff, friends, and subscribers of Identity Network—I could never have done it without you. Lastly, this book is dedicated to my Lord and Savior, Jesus, who has always shown His unconditional love toward me and the whole world.

Acknowledgments

I want to acknowledge Mike Morrell, Brittian Bullock, and Betsy Zabel for helping to put together this book and staying up late to get the job done. You're the best, my friends! Also, I want to thank Destiny Image for giving me the opportunity to publish this book.

Endorsements

In a season like this, we need sound prophetic ministry that flows from the mercy seat rather than the judgment seat. Prophetic ministry established in present truth and recognizing due order is not always easy to find, but such is the ministry of Jeremy Lopez.

Bishop David Huskins
Senior Pastor, Cedar Lake Christian Center

Identity Network is doing a great job of creating a hunger and thirst for the supernatural move of the Holy Spirit. Jeremy Lopez is one of the next generation prophetic voices that God clearly has His hand on! You will receive grounded teaching and inspiring prophetic activity, and you will get to observe integrity at work. It is my honor to be a friend of this ministry.

James W. Goll
Founder, Encounters Network

I've been blessed to minister alongside Jeremy Lopez. I love his passion. I love the word of God in him, and I see the love that shines through him from the Father and Jesus Christ to the Body. He encourages, he exhorts, and he brings comfort with clarity with his prophetic gift. You will be greatly blessed by Jeremy Lopez.

Julie Meyer
International House of Prayer

I love Jeremy Lopez's passion to see the Body of Christ encouraged. He carries a dynamic word, is extremely accurate in his prophetic ministry, and is a true refreshment to those whose lives he touches.

Patricia King
www.XPmedia.com

Contents

Living in I AM

There is nothing more exciting than the revelation of the Eternal "Now-ness" of God. God transcends time and space and is eternal; yet He brings eternity into the now at all times. He cannot be confined to time; yet He shows up in time and always in the time known as now. He was the God who appeared yesterday, but when He was there, it was now. He will be the God who appears tomorrow, but by that time it will be now. How can a God of eternity live in the now? To answer that, we must discover one of the most amazing attributes of God and that is His own announcement, "I AM that I AM" (Exod. 3:14).

Jeremy Lopez has undertaken the task in this Christo-centric treatise to unveil not only the I AM, but how we as believers can live in the I AM in the now. To learn of Christ as the I AM is to learn of ourselves living in the now. If God is the God who is, was, and shall forever be, then it is clear that He always manifests in the now to address our past and to secure our future.

If we are to live in the now, we must become intimately acquainted with the I AM. He is not a theory we read about or a concept we have thought about. He is the great I AM. In this book, Jeremy Lopez points out that a great part of getting to know the I AM is about unlearning. As he states in his writing, when we recognize the immediacy of I AM, suddenly something new is required of us too! We then must change to embrace a new understanding of the power of that moment. That requires a certain amount of unlearning.

In essence, as the author so clearly establishes, for those of us who are redeemed, "time is an illusion when it comes to our nature as sons and daughters of God." If we are living in the one who is the I AM, then we are always living in an Eternal Now. Faith is now. The Kingdom is now. Salvation is now. We live in the now because we live in the I AM.

I commend this book to every serious seeker of truth. Jeremy has, with a prophetic edge, taken us one step closer to seeing life from God's perspective. He also has interwoven quotes from both sacred and secular scholars that provoke thought on time and eternity and what happens when eternity invades time. I think it is time to live in the now by living in the I AM.

I rejoice that every day more and more light is being revealed and I AM is being seen. As you read this book, may you determine to never again live in a lesser realm of having instead of being and never again live from a past or future focus when you can live in the now. I know now living is attainable because we have I AM living in us—so perhaps it is time we live in Him.

David Huskins
Presiding Archbishop
International Communion of Charismatic Churches

Explanation of Spiritual Exercises

You can know and experience God in the present moment, here and now, as you work, eat and drink, sleep, raise your children, and encounter life as it is. That is the main thrust of this book. In a way, I'll simply be taking different stabs at this reality, attempting to convey this fairly simple theme in a myriad of ways until one of them speaks to you. One of the ways I'm hoping to engage you, the reader, is through very practical—and practicable—actions. Like any adventurer or explorer will tell you, it's one thing to see something on a map; it's entirely something else to encounter the territory in real life. This is why I feel that it's imperative for our spiritual development that we make use of what have, for centuries, been known as "spiritual exercises."

If you're like me, the word *exercises* makes you think of squats, bench presses, and looking ridiculous trying to do a push-up "the right way." Truthfully, in the past I haven't liked the idea of exercises because it makes a demand of me. It forces me to stick with something regular. It forces me to attempt something I might not be able to do. And quite honestly, there's nothing worse than failing at yet *another* goal. That's why so many people cease making New Year's resolutions. They just don't want to fail again.

Sadly, most people think of spiritual "routines" or exercises in these same terms. We have been conditioned to envision them as the core of the Christian life. We have been taught that Bible reading, Sunday school and church attendance, giving, devotional readings, and various forms of prayer (largely asking God for things) are the backbone of Christianity. This is simply not the case.

Union with God through Jesus Christ is the centerpiece of the faith. Nothing more and nothing less. How faithful you are at attending religious services bears little reflection on your union with the Divine, nor does how early you get up to read your Bible. To equate those elements with our level of intimacy with God is a minimization of the overwhelming God we serve. Far from being the root of the life of faith, those activities are merely scaffolding by which the actual object may be constructed. In other words, they're not the main act!

Any form of exercise may be thought of as preparation for the possible. A runner who trains daily finds herself capable of participating in a race. She may not even be aware of a race coming. She might be taken completely unawares. However, the consistent exercise that she has submitted herself to has prepared her—it's brought her up to speed.

In a similar sense, a scientist uses experiments to draw data leading him toward a hypothesis. The main point isn't the experiment. Oh, it's helpful. It's certainly useful. It may prove or disprove certain elements that he had assumed. It will undoubtedly assist, but its ultimate purpose is as a means to an end. Because of this, interestingly, there's really no such thing as a failed experiment, save one that doesn't occur—one that never gets off the ground. In truth, any results that one gets from an experiment simply further the objective, which is knowledge—or awareness of what's really going on. I think this is a wonderful way to envision spiritual exercises. They are both training for what is to come, but also a wonderful means of seeing what *is*.

Consider this scenario: Imagine you're sitting attempting to focus on God, but instead you are distracted by thoughts about your budget, thoughts about your rent, thoughts about your children. You smell the smoke drifting through the air from a neighbor's fireplace. You feel your hands grow sweaty. At the end of your ten-minute session you get up, exasperated! *This has been useless*, you think! *What a waste of time.*

Or was it? What's there to feel exasperated about anyway? The goal was simply to see what would happen if you set aside ten minutes to focus on God. You did just that. And now you know. What exactly do you know? You know that today, on such and such day of such and such month in such and such year at such and such time, in this particular place you thought more about financial obligations than anything else. And that's interesting. Make a note of this. Then move on. You found what you came for! Now, onto the next experiment.

Isn't this wonderful? How freeing! When we approach spiritual exercise as a grand experiment—taking note of what happens and recognizing that it is assisting us and preparing us for the real work of loving union with the Divine—then we are free to truly have fun!

It's a strange thought, isn't it? Routine, discipline, experiment, or exercise as adventure. But that is exactly what it is when we liberate ourselves from the judgment of imagining that we have to get it right. There's nothing to get right. The most important thing to God is that we desire to spend time with Him, that we are His. And this is exactly what these disciplines are: exercises in creating space for God's presence.

As you read through the chapters, you'll see that an experiment of some sort is at the end of each one. I hope you'll consider attempting these exercises, and perhaps as you do you might eventually integrate them into your life. I have adapted many of these "action steps" from ancient and modern sources—skilled explorers of the spirit who have gone before us. These pathways, well worn by our spiritual ancestors, can aid us greatly in our pursuit of "practicing God's presence."

However, even if you do not utilize these specific exercises, my encouragement to you is that you not be complacent, simply reading the words of this book, but that you actually convert it into living. As a dear friend mentioned once, "If you wish to know yourself, be awake, practice awareness. If you wish to be yourself... ACT!" And that is the thought behind the exercises throughout this book. Be yourself. Wear your own skin, here and now. Be caught in the presence of the Eternal I AM—and don't procrastinate! Do it today.

Living in the I AM
Exercise One: Keeping a Journal

Let's do one exercise before you even dive into the meat of this book. Starting as soon as you can, keep a record of your experiences, insights, and revelations that occur as you read and act on the thoughts presented in this book. Journaling is only a tool for becoming more self-aware, for awakening. Journals can be a powerful reminder, as we draw together the strands of past experience and future hopes into an active engagement of the present moment. They can cause us to see ourselves as ever-changing creatures, constantly being rearranged in the wake of both the mundane and miraculous.

Your first entry might be a highly personal confession of where you begin this exploratory journey. What are your hopes and fears? Why did you choose this particular book? What about this topic draws you and calls to you? Where are you in your current life situation? What is your present story? Are there threads of triumph, despair, struggle, doubt, joy, or sorrow? What are some specific memories that represent these elements?

In future journal entries, respond to the questions located at the end of the chapters. Don't feel as if you must directly answer them, but rather let them impact you and take you places, allowing the Spirit to guide you into all truth. Also include your reactions to the variety of exercises suggested and attempted throughout the book. Your responses can be as lengthy or as brief as you desire.

You can use the journal in any form that you want. It can be linear and linguistic, such as a normal diary. Or it could be completely visual, utilizing pictures, cutouts, and objects to convey your reactions. The point is not to limit how God's creative giftings flow through you.

When I journal, I find it useful to clear my mind first, to let all the clutter and the "noise of the day" fall off me. If you can do a little "chimney sweeping" (as Freud called it), then you can inhabit a space where you are most responsive to God and able to spontaneously respond to where your spirit, in tune with the Holy Spirit, is taking you.

There isn't an audience here save only you and your Lord. Let this be an honest record of your approach to living in the Present, in the Now.

A Word About Sources

In this book I will be drawing on a wide range of parables, stories, and written sources. Many of these will come from the Jewish and Christian heritage common to many readers—but I don't stop there. I engage material from Buddhist, Hindu, and contemporary spiritual sources, and I understand that this might raise some eyebrows. Please understand that fundamental to my outlook on sources is a question: *Not* "Does this come from 'approved' or 'insider' channels?" but "Is this true? Real? Helpful? God-illumining?"

I feel like I have biblical precedent for this kind of litmus test, versus the kind that religious gatekeepers often employ. In his famous meeting with esteemed pagan philosophers at Mars Hill in Greece, the apostle Paul was emboldened to see divine revelation in the "unauthorized" (pagan) poetry of his day. He approvingly quoted this moving verse back to them, speaking of God: *"In Him we live, and move, and have our being"* (Acts 17:28). He didn't shy away from truth because of its source—because Paul knew, ultimately, that there is but one source for all truth.

I believe that Jesus has a special place in His heart for spiritual outsiders. A group of Bedouin magicians recognized the infant Jesus—when many of His own faith didn't—and presented Him with gifts (see Matt. 2:1-12). Jesus fellowshipped with the heretical Samaritan women with no preconditions (see John 4) and extolled the Samaritan people as the pinnacle of love and virtue in one of his most famous parables (see Luke 10:25-37). It is God's will to draw *all* people to Himself in greater God-consciousness (see John 12:32), which I believe comes as we learn to practice God's presence in the Eternal Now. God is no respecter of persons or sources—wisdom speaks from the most unlikely places.

This does not mean that I demean Christian orthodoxy. I fully affirm the Scriptures of both Old and New Testaments as the ultimate revelation, and the Apostles' and Nicene Creeds form the bedrock of my faith as a follower of God in the Way of Jesus. But I believe that being solidly rooted is the first step in *branching out* to become the people Jesus is forming us to be—scandalously available to absolutely everyone and radically inclusive regarding where we hear the Spirit's voice of wisdom.

And so, with Bible in hand and Spirit-birthed discernment in your heart, I invite you to follow me beyond the charismatic clichés and religious rote into a genuinely fresh adventure of present-tense living!

CHAPTER ONE

The Eternal Now

I am as sure as I live that nothing is so near to me as God. God is nearer to me than I am to myself; my existence depends on the nearness and the presence of God.

—Meister Eckhart[1]

Every moment is crammed with infinite riches which are given us according to the extent of our faith and love.

—Jean-Pierre de Caussade[2]

The secret of health for both mind and body is not to mourn for the past, nor to worry about the future, but to live the present moment wisely and earnestly.

—Buddha[3]

Knowing God means living in the Eternal Now. Most of us, though we probably aren't aware of it, trudge along pining for a past that is no more or agonizing about a future that does not yet exist. In other words, we're living in a dream world! We dream of yesterday when things were "better," when life was less complicated. We dream of making different decisions than the ones we've made. We have nightmares of regret and guilt. We spend our waking hours dreaming about what's next, about our projected hopes and retroactive fears. Hardly really living at all, life passes us by. We mature, we go off to school, perhaps get married, and have children. We grow old, and then we die, never having lived *right now*, in the present moment. The wonder of creation, the beauty of human existence, and the full presence of God are lost on us.

We grow old, and then we die, never having lived *right now*, **in the present moment.**

I heard a story about a Chinese general who had been given command of the king's forces before a major battle. His friends and soldiers threw a celebration for him, and the festivities extended late into the night.

The sounds from the party were so loud that they woke the king, who instantly became angry. He thought to himself that the general must be a man of low character and wasn't suited to be his commander. The king then dispatched his guards to inform the general that he would be executed the following day, which they did. When the general heard the news, his face became very serious; he was inwardly terrified. Then the words of his wise master came to mind. "Tomorrow is not real. The only reality is now."

And so he came into the present—as he did, he began to laugh, then dance with all his might. The guards were bewildered at what was happening and went back to report the curious turn of events to the king, who determined to go see this madman for himself. When he came into the celebration there, he saw the general, enjoying himself thoroughly. "What is the meaning of this? Who celebrates on the eve of their death?" the king demanded.

His soon-to-be-executed general then told him that as a soldier he had always lived knowing that he could die at any minute, but death had seemed remote and only a possibility. But when he received word that he would most certainly die the next day, he lost all fear of the future—for it has ceased to exist outside the next several hours. He had realized the truth of his master's statement (that the only moment he had was this one) and had decided to experience it and enjoy fully. The king was amazed, not only sparing the general, but also becoming his disciple.

A present reality and an awareness of living in the now means abandoning personal assumptions in order to gain something far greater and more life-giving.

This parable's meaning seems clear. It teaches us the importance of living in the moment, or in "the Now." The initial response you may have is acknowledgment of the story, but what does it matter to you, in your daily life? This can be answered by asking what "living in the Now" *meant* for the general or the king? For the general, it meant constant joy and peace in the face of fear and death. For the king, it was a catalyst for redemption and hope. A present reality and an awareness of living in the now means abandoning personal assumptions in order to gain something far greater and more life-giving.

A Timely Question

God exists in the eternals, which is exactly where we are called to live as well. *"God raised us up with Christ and seated us with Him in the heavenly realms in Christ Jesus,"* the apostle Paul writes (Eph. 2:6 NIV). But most humans I've encountered live by *time*. Sometimes it seems like our favorite game is inventing the future. It's actually a form of escape from having to exist in the Now—where God is. Time, like a cruel joke, teases us into thinking that we can change ourselves bit by bit, just a little a day. Gradually, we imagine, we can be at peace. This is wishful thinking at best. By existing in the Now of God, we must act. We have to come to a place of repentance and transformation *today*.

Just think of that for a moment. There's a real problem to our well-laid plans if time were to just disappear. Action is suddenly necessary. But often we don't want to deal with our many problems, so we look at the clock and "invent time" as a way to avoid dealing with them. *Time is an illusion when it comes to our nature as Sons and Daughters of God.* We are children of God, now! We are forgiven, now! We are more than conquerors, now! We are holy, chosen, beloved, accepted, redeemed, justified, and cleansed, now! These are not future wishes and dreams. These are not time-based actions. These are realities of our true identity in Christ, and they are found in the Now.

 Time is an illusion when it comes to our nature as Sons and Daughters of God.

As people of faith, hope, and love, the single greatest question we may ask is this:

"What is the Spirit doing right now?"

Truthfully, I believe that most of God's people really *want* to know the answer to this. We instinctually *want* to be in the center of God's will. It's in our spiritual DNA to be fully present and fully at home with the direction of the Holy Spirit. This longing can be felt all across the world today. It's the topic of countless articles and books; hundreds of conferences address this as their point, and a multitude of sermons hope to direct us there. Sadly, the solutions offered are often ineffective. They are Band-Aids, counterfeits of God's ultimate intention that we exist in the absolute present.

If Only We Could Go Back...

The Church is experiencing an identity crisis. Dwindling congregations and shrinking budgets have left many church leaders frantically searching for solutions—ways to fill in the gap, to make it one more Sunday. There are more than enough of these temporary fixes to choose from. Some point backward toward the traditions or experiences of the past. Think of the last time you went to your local Christian bookstore. Do you remember the titles you saw? Without calling attention to specific authors, I can tell you that there is a widespread obsession with "going backward." It's not unlike the old joke about bad country music, "I want my dog back, I want my family back, I want my job back...." In the Church this translates into God's people looking over their shoulders at yesterday for inspiration, instruction, and outright imitation.

There are movements that enshrine the early Church, searching the New Testament for some hidden historical message of Jesus and the apostles for today, or aim to set up some carbon copy of First Century conditions. Others delve even further, trying to add Torah observance and Jewish culture to their holy To-Do list. For still others, this isn't backward-looking enough: Like Nicodemus, they wonder if they should crawl back into the "Womb" of humanity—they want to go back to Eden!

Just today I read an article in a high profile magazine that hinted at a discovery of a lost prayer that had been used exclusively by the initial believers in Jesus. The piece went on to tell its readers exactly what words had been used in those ages past and how we could use them now. We speak about Jesus living 2,000 years ago and the historical precedents of the apostles. We make ourselves historians of Jesus of Nazareth. We study ancient Jewish culture and research Roman crucifixions to better understand our Savior's life and death. And while this can be fine and good, as we engage this line of thinking, we may exchange reliance on the living Spirit of God for ashy rote words and dry intellectual bones.

Placing our hope in past practices or understandings is both seductive and deceptive. We are lured into believing that God's best—His Plan A—already came and went and that today is just a recovery operation— Plan B. This is an easy trap to fall into. And while we would never acknowledge it out loud, many of our unspoken beliefs support this thought.

The lie of the enemy that suggests we are just a part of a practice run is false.

But God's Eternal Purpose was never centered on Adam; it is centered in the person of Jesus Christ. And now, through the Holy Spirit, it is squarely aimed at you and me. God had a kind and loving desire that was never detoured or railroaded. He is always on the move. He is new every morning. He is the ever-present Now, the Great I AM, the Eternal Word. The lie of the enemy that suggests we are just a part of a practice run is false.

We are standing in the great hour of God's good will. The mind of Christ is our freely offered gift *now*, if we'll just enter in. We cannot afford to be deceived by feelings that imagine the past as something better than God's best, which is always housed in the Now.

Looking for a Better Tomorrow

Beyond dredging the past 2,000 years for a sense of direction, there is also a form of spiritual fortune-telling that is becoming commonplace. Trend-watching is a rising tide within the Church. Congregations everywhere are changing formats, redesigning their identities, and pandering to their surrounding culture, not on the basis of God's Spirit and His Word, but rather on potential future trends. Once again this substitutes faddism and mental acrobatics for discernment and trust in God's deep investment in the here and now.

If we're not obsessing about current flavor-of-the-week crowd-entertainment tactics, we are stubbornly yearning for the *Some*day of the Lord—when Christ will return to rescue His Bride and redeem His Church and set all things right. We wait for the day and sing songs about the clouds being rolled back like a scroll. We watch for the antichrist on the nightly news, and start seeing weather patterns as divine acts of judgment. We invite our coworkers to special revival meetings and pray, "Prepare ye the way of the Lord." As believers we must solidly recognize that Jesus's words instructing His disciples that "no one knows the day nor the hour" (see Mark 13:32; Matt. 24:36-44) were words of freedom. He was telling us to put away the crystal ball.

Jesus understood that worrying about tomorrow really doesn't do much good. The data is never all in. There are endless variables and limitless possibilities. In fact, with the God of "all things are possible," we can expect the unexpected. In other words, we have no idea what God has in store for the next moment. Thus, worrying about the future is an exercise in futility. Our hope comes in laying aside our fear of what may be and releasing ourselves into the all-knowing and all-compassionate hands of our Lord. Truthfully Jesus's words have always summed this up for me, "Let tomorrow worry about itself" (see Matt. 6:34). We are called to live in the Eternal *I AM* of God.

Living in the Now

All of God's efforts, the entirety of His work in the world and in us as individuals, is enacted in the present moment. In fact the Now is not only the instrument of God's design, but it is also His purpose as well. God's kind intention is to open our eyes to the joy set before us, the Kingdom that is right at hand—in front of us. He's always drawing and calling us to exist in His Right-nowness.

All of God's efforts, the entirety of His work in the world and in us as individuals, is enacted in the present moment.

The relevant question that we, as Christians, must continue to come back to is what I mentioned earlier: Where is Jesus now? The answer is quite simple: *The Christ who lives within us, is in this simple and unadorned moment.*

We cannot afford to dismiss the provocative notion that there is an Eternal Present in which we live—the same Eternal Present of Jesus. The Eternal Present is the only space in which your life unfolds. It is the only place where there is life. This is the only moment you have. Stop dreaming. Stop living in unreality. We must begin to live in the now.

The Power to Live in the Present

In order to live in the center of God's will, we have to let reverberate through our souls the same name of God that Moses forsook past and future to receive:

That name of course is Yahweh—the I AM.

This reminds me of the teacher who was giving a talk on modern inventions:

"Are there any of you who can mention something of importance that has never before existed except in the last twenty years?" she asked.

An especially smart boy in the front row lifted his hand and eagerly said, "What God is doing in me!"[4]

I can tell you to live in the now, and I can tell you it's important, but until you understand the "why" for yourself, you will not go far. I invite you to be present in the pages of this book, that you would join me in discovering the power of Now.

Questions to Ponder

If time is a matter of perspective, a human-made construct, how does that change the way you view it? ___

_____

_____

_____

What kind of thinker are you? Do you tend to wait for the future, or do you dwell in the past? Can you even recognize what the Now looks like? _____

_____

_____

_____

_____

What is the Spirit doing right now? Where is the Spirit? Spend some time on this one. Think about this in terms of relationships, places, emotions, and actions. _____

_____

_____

_____

_____

Why does it matter? Do some soul-searching. Do you desire to be in step with the Spirit? Why or why not?

_____

_____

_____

Living in the I AM
Exercise Two: Contemplation

In the real work of the spirit, our minds can only take us so far. Imagine a relay race in which the mind hands off to the heart—filled with the energy of emotions and intuition—who then, in turn, makes the pass to our actual deeds. It requires all three working in tandem to win the race.

Reading the Scripture for study can bring deep insight, inspiration, and humility. The words become carriers of truth into our minds and hearts. However, words processed only through study can easily become dry ash to our spirits. We must come to a place beyond words.

When we calm ourselves, stilling our thoughts for just a moment, we come to a place of openness to God's voice, and God's person. *"Be still, and know that I am God"* (Ps. 46:10). In other words, as we still ourselves, we come to an experiential knowing or oneness with the I AM. We place ourselves in position to encounter the Eternal Now. As Madam Jean Guyon, the 14th-century Catholic mystic said, that there comes a moment in all believers' lives when they must put aside the things of the world for the things of God. Still later we must even put aside the things of God for God Himself.[5] It is with this in mind that we cease our speaking *at* God or our studying *of* God and focus on becoming still before God, beholding His beauty. True contemplation is true prayer, absolute union with God.

Contemplation Exercise 1

Begin your contemplation early in the day if possible. Choose a verse or passage from Scripture that seems meaningful to you in this moment (not just one that has historically mattered), that touches the center of your being. Read the portion a few times. Wrestle with what it might mean in your head. Then read it once more and just bathe in it—don't use the mind to understand it. Allow it to fall on you. If you'd like to, repeat this step.

During the rest of your day, whenever you find yourself becoming distracted, worried, busied, hurried, or simply in need of living in the Now, remember this verse from the Bible and let it take hold of you once more.

Beyond meditating on Scripture, feel free to contemplate other elements that draw your attention to God's person. Creation, the gentle ripple of a stream, the wind blowing the trees, a truly divine quality such as compassion or grace, or even a hub-bub of people are all things that can remind of us God.

Contemplation Exercise 2

Sit quietly for ten minutes. Divide a page in your journal into two sections: PAST and FUTURE. List all your thoughts under those two headings during that time. Consider how many of your thoughts fall under one of these two categories.

CHAPTER TWO

Stuck in a Moment

The time of business does not with me differ from the time of prayer, and in the noise and clatter of my kitchen, while several persons are at the same time calling for different things, I possess God as if I were upon my knees at the blessed sacrament.

—Brother Lawrence[1]

If you are weary of some sleepy form of devotion, probably God is as weary of it as you are.

—Frank Laubach[2]

Come, then, my beloved souls, let us fly to
that love which calls us.
Why are we waiting?
Let us set out at once,
Let us lose ourselves in the very heart of God
and become intoxicated with His love.
Let us snatch from His heart the key to all
the treasures of the world and start out right
away on the road to heaven.
There is no need to fear that any lock will
hold us back.
Our key will open every door.
There is no room we cannot enter.
We can make ourselves free of the garden, the
cellar, and the vineyard as well.
If we want to explore the countryside, no one
will hinder us.
We can come and go;
We can enter and leave any place we wish,
Because we have the key of David, the key of
knowledge, and the key of the abyss that holds
the hidden treasures of divine wisdom.
It is this key that opens the doors of mystical
death and its sacred darkness.
By it we can enter the deepest dungeons and
emerge safe and sound.
It gives us entrance into that blessed spot
where the light of knowledge shines and
the Bridegroom takes His noonday rest.
—Jean-Pierre de Caussade[3]

Remember leaving home for the first time? For some of us, it was going off to college, or on an extended missions trip, or maybe just moving out and growing into adulthood. All of us, at some point, experience change in our home—in the place we rely upon the most. Regardless of how it happened, the moment is usually pretty significant to most people. A friend of mine remembers helping his older brother move into his college dorm; when it came time to leave, their father broke down in body-heaving sobs. It was the first time he had ever seen his father cry.

Leaving home means escaping the safe arms of the familiar, and—at least, in our culture—it means finding some degree of independence. For some of us, it translates into being woken up by harsh realities. We face something we hadn't expected, that we weren't prepared for. The beliefs we received from our parents are challenged. The tools that used to build the architecture of our lives simply don't construct anything meaningful anymore.

Have you realized yet that the Holy Spirit comes upon us in precisely these moments? This is the Heavenly Workman's bench for renovating our hearts. Consider this: Saul of Tarsus was *stuck* in a past-based religious persona that was suffocating him. Smugly confident in his interpretations of Law and decorum, his wedded-ness to yesterday's glory was producing *lethal* fruit: namely, killing and persecuting followers of the Way up and down Asia Minor. It is here that Luke tells us, in Acts, that *now* interrupts Saul's stuff: **"Suddenly...***from heaven...***"** (Acts 9:3). It was in the *suddenly, from heaven* that the *"bright light from heaven"* shone down and blinded Saul's natural eyes so that his inner eye could be illuminated (see Acts 22:6 NIV; Matt. 6:22). He saw Jesus and knew what he *now* must do. "Suddenly, from heaven!" became a radical reorientation that changed his very name from Saul to Paul and has reverberated in our lives ever since.

If we recognize the immediacy of *I AM*, *suddenly*, something *new* is required from us, too!

Both Luke and Mark use this word, *suddenly,* many times to describe the motion of the Spirit as well as the work of Jesus and God's surprising Kingdom. It's impossible to escape the fact that the Gospel writers—those closest to Jesus—were impacted by the ***interrupting*** *realit*y of God in their lives. If we recognize the immediacy of *I AM, suddenly,* something *new* is required from us, too! We are forced to improvise, to change our habits, and to listen to the Spirit right now. In other words, we wake up.

The whole process is, in a word, all about *unlearning.* True spirituality, true religion, is a willingness to unlearn everything we thought we knew. Having a relationship with God in reality is putting aside the past and stepping into freedom from the known. It is unlearning the limitations of the past and stepping into the now.

I often think of the story of Abraham, the father of the faithful. His whole life is like a living parable about following God out of the past and into the new thing that God promised to do. When we first meet him, he's called by the name *Abram* and is living in the land of his ancestry. He's worshiping the old gods of Ur. He's drawing from hundreds of years of religious and cultural experience. He's going through the same old rituals. He's living in the past. For him the past is a wheelchair. He's moving, he's able to get around, he's going from this place to that, but he's limited. The past is an object that is limiting God's dealings in his life.

But then God speaks to him. Borrowing from what we already saw with the writers of the New Testament, I'm sure that God's voice came *suddenly.* It interrupted his world. His instructions are to *"Go from your country, your people and your father's household to the land I will show you"* (Gen. 12:1 NIV) The significance of these words is difficult to overemphasize. God is inviting Abram to move beyond the known and the knowable, and into the risk-filled, perilous, and Spirit-saturated present moment. God is saying, imperatively, "Get up! Get out of the wheelchair of the past and walk, run, and soar into the presence of what I am doing now!"

God is saying, imperatively, "Get up! Get out of the wheelchair of the past and walk, run, and soar into the presence of what I am doing now!"

This is exactly what God calls us to do throughout the rest of Scripture. The fact that Jesus called His disciples while out on a walk and they dropped everything they were doing to follow Him should shake us a good deal. We need to realize that we are not dealing with a past-tense-dwelling God!

Living in the present moment changes us. It changes us from Saul to Paul, and here once again, from Abram to Abraham. A shift happens at the core of our being when we commit ourselves to practice God's present-tense *presence*; a synching with the Spirit occurs, where our spirits can say with God's Spirit, "I am!" Just as Paul and Abraham were renamed, we are remade in God's presence.

Until this moment we will find ourselves like Abram at Ur—in ways that are perhaps uncomfortable to admit. The land of our fathers from which we are called is a familiar place. It represents the cycles of the past, the circles of previous events. Some of those moments are positive. They are places of significance. They are Sunday morning services where we've been overwhelmed with a special sense of God's presence. They are weeks at Bible camp and Sunday dinner after church. They are mountaintops and prayer closets. Our pasts that are so familiar are often beautiful and routinely blessed.

But the land of our fathers is also a place of sadness. It can be a place of hurt and sorrow, a place of guilt from previous errors or the remorse we are left with after thoughtless actions—whether they are our own or someone else's—and sins of the past, generational curses, shadows of what could have been and what we might have improved had we only been given the opportunity. Whether glowing and glittery or haunting and humiliating, the land of the past is the place that the faithful are compelled to leave because we have been promised something greater.

 Whether glowing and glittery or haunting and humiliating, the land of the past is the place that the faithful are compelled to leave because we have been promised something greater.

It's funny and sad how much of our lives we spend thinking about the past. Take, for example, when something happens and we get hurt. Immediately we exhaust ourselves, tensed against that particular experience. We replay the moment over and over. *I can't believe she said that to me* or *I will never forget the look on his face when I told him.* It's on repeat in our minds. Our stance becomes one where we are determined not to get burned again by *that* situation. Here's the tragedy, though: We are in fact far more cruel than our offenders: They only slandered us once, but we do it to ourselves over and over again in the theaters of our minds!

This reminds me of an oft-told parable. Two monks were walking from one village to another. On the way they came to a large stream that they had to cross. At the brink of the puddle they saw a young woman standing, afraid to cross it.

"Come," said one of the monks, "I will carry you to the other side." He took her on his back, and carried her to the other side of the puddle.

After crossing the road, the two monks continued walking silently for hours, until they reached their destination.

The other monk could not keep silent any longer and exclaimed: "You know we're not supposed to have anything to do with women, and you picked that woman up and carried her across the stream!"

The monk who carried the woman over the puddle smiled and said: "I picked her up and set her down. You have been carrying her all this way."[4]

This is present awareness contrasted with living in the past.

Whenever we find ourselves "stuck in a moment," there *is* a way out. We can access the infinite grace and compassion that God shines through Jesus if we but allow ourselves a simple realization:

- It already happened.

- It's already over.

- That very particular moment will never happen again.

- Other moments will. Something else will happen.

Try it!

Sadly, we're usually too busy looking at what just happened to be attentive to what's *happening* in the here and now. It is so simple to live protecting ourselves against the experience we just had, blinding us to the wonders of now. Learning the simple, grace-enabling exercise above is part of what it means to be free from the burdens of the past. God is calling us to cease living in what I call "Instant Replay" mode. Memories (both positive and negative) on "Instant Replay" might be good for the game of football, but not the game of life. After all: Who needs to see that fumble, in slow motion, three times with those highlighter arrows?

 God is calling us to cease living in "Instant Replay" mode.

The same is also true of positive experiences from the past. We can be so wrapped up in idolizing what has been, waiting for the moment to reoccur, that we fail to see the new thing that God wishes to do. *"Behold I am doing a **new** thing…do you not perceive it?"* says the Lord (Isa. 43:19 RSV). And the answer is an overwhelming *no* in many of our lives—we don't perceive it. We are too busy wishing for what was, patterning our lives to what has just been, that we fail to notice God's goodness streaming through the desert of our lives.

Focus is a precious gift—it can only be spent in one place at a time. When we focus our attention on the past, we are turning our faces away from the present. We can't be in two places at once. But what is most troublesome about this is that the past is dead. If we are choosing to live in the past, we are essentially choosing death, necrophilia, gazing on a corpse. When we dwell in the past, we are deliberately rejecting Jesus's offering of abundant life and a life to the fullest. *"Let the dead bury their own dead,"* Jesus said (Matt. 8:22 NKJV). We would do well to heed!

If we are choosing to live in the past, we are essentially choosing death, necrophilia, gazing on a corpse.

We have to stop living in, focusing on, and reacting to the past. Isaiah gives the people of Israel God's perspective when he said, *"See, the former things have taken place, and new things I declare…. Forget the former things; do not dwell on the past. See, I am doing a new thing"* (Isa. 42:9; 43:18-19a NIV).

I'll be honest: It's terrifying to expect the unexpected. We don't want the new thing. We are like our forefathers running out of Egypt with breathless abandon, ecstatic to be released, jubilant over our recently discovered freedom, only to begin complaining in the desert, pining after our captors, and romanticizing slavery. We rationalize that at least in Egypt, we knew what to expect. At least in Egypt, life made sense. Yet in the desert of life, we follow a cloud around aimlessly. We wait for food to drop down from the sky every morning, and for what? Why can't we just go back to what was familiar? The freedom and uncontrollability of the present is frustrating to us.

Yet it is here, in absolute dependence on the Spirit of God, that we are called to live. In the desert—which symbolizes how we often encounter life as halfway between where God is taking us and where He is redeeming us from—we begin to encounter the Lord as He is. We receive God as radical provision for the moment. We watch Him transform our circumstances by interrupting our well-thought-out plans. He becomes everything real and true to us.

There in the desert we are given new names. We are re-created in the image of God, having shed the baggage of the land of our fathers, and now living by a new life. No longer are we seated; we are walking—running—and finally find our feet no longer touching the ground.

Questions to Ponder

Think about your childhood and growing years. Were they good or bad? Do you wish to repeat them, or do you wish to forget them? How might this influence you today? _____

_____

_____

Are there circumstances in your life that you are "stuck" on? Are there stories you watch on "Instant Replay?"

_____

_____

What events of change are significant in your life? Try to list up to five of them. What were your reactions to them? Were they negative or positive? _____

_____

_____

_____

Have you experienced the "suddenness" of God in those moments? As you reflect on these events through the lens of "God's interruptions," what do you see? _____

_____

_____

_____

Are there desert seasons in your life? What might be a desert in your life right now? _____

_____

_____

What is God's response to your desert? What is your "manna"? How might He be redeeming this desert place? _____

_____

_____

Living in the I AM
Exercise Three: Bearing Witness

The thoughts that you are thinking right now are quite simply a fragment of what's actually going on in your head. Behind those conscious parts of yourself are incredible and expansive unconscious, highly conditioned ways of being you. Most of the things that we just accept as "who we are" exist at this level. We rarely think about them. From time to time we encounter a glimpse of our selves, but are quickly pulled away by distracting forces.

The practice of developing an inner witness is an ancient one, but with highly biblical roots as well. As we are joined to the Lord, we have been made one Spirit with Him (see 1 Cor. 6:17). The Spirit Himself witnesses to our spirits. As God views us, we are able to receive a sanctified vision of our selves. When this happens, many of the unconscious roadblocks to our lives with God disappear, and we are able to live more fully in His divine reality.

Bearing witness means simply observing. The witness isn't there to judge, isn't there to critique or evaluate. When we bear witness, we simply notice what's going on inside of ourselves. Here's an example: If you get into a fight with your spouse and then go gorge yourself on ice cream afterward, and end the night by beating yourself up for having eaten so much, the witness would note: He ate quite a bit of ice cream and he put himself down for doing so. It sounds a little strange to talk about yourself as another person doesn't it? But actually this little step is very helpful. It reminds us that we are, at our core, so much bigger than our actions or even the unconscious motives behind them.

Why not try it? Cultivate a practice of allowing the Spirit to flow into your spirit, informing you about *you*. What are you thinking right now? What are your actions right now? And so on... Try to pass no judgment. Try not to consider what category your motives fall into. Simply watch. Listen. Accept.

CHAPTER THREE

The Worries of Tomorrow

To be identified with your mind is to be trapped in time: the compulsion to live almost exclusively through memory and anticipation.

—Eckhart Tolle[1]

The day you are happy for no reason whatsoever, the day you find yourself taking delight in everything and in nothing, you will know that you have found the land of unending joy called the kingdom.

—Anthony de Mello[2]

I drove away from my mind everything capable of spoiling the sense of the presence of God.... I

just make it my business to persevere in His holy
presence... My soul has had an habitual, silent,
secret conversation with God.

—Brother Lawrence[3]

If you've ever been in college, odds are you are extremely familiar with the following scenario. It is your freshman year and you are home for Christmas. Your Aunt Carol and Uncle John are there with your 12 cousins and your grandparents. Your dad starts trimming the Christmas ham, and before you can even pass the mashed potatoes, Aunt Carol asks, "So what are you studying?"

"Communications," you say evenly.

"Oh—and what are you going to do with that?" she inquires with complete confusion.

Meanwhile, your entire family stares at you with open curiosity, fully expecting an answer as to how you are going to spend the next 30 years of your life.

It is one of the most frustrating moments for an 18-21 year old. Whether they know what they want to do or not, the question illustrates an interesting assumption in our culture.

There is no aspect of life we don't wish to control, plan for, or worry about.

We want to plan for everything, good and bad. We are planning for the future. We are looking ahead. We are devising a five-year plan. We are plotting our next career move—every contingency accounted for. We meet with financial advisors to set up our Roth IRA's and 401k's. We diversify our portfolios. This can be a positive way of looking at the future—stockpiling or investing our money. Yet our negative side can get the best of us. We buy life insurance policies. We have elaborate contracts for personal and general coverage, liability, worker's compensation, and even "acts of God." There is no aspect of life we don't wish to control, plan for, or worry about.

Jesus told a story about this once.

He [Jesus] told them this parable: "The ground of a certain rich man yielded an abundant harvest. He thought to himself, 'What shall I do? I have no place to store my crops.'

"Then he said, 'This is what I'll do. I will tear down my barns and build bigger ones, and there I will store my surplus grain. And I'll say to myself, "You have plenty of grain laid up for many years. Take life easy; eat, drink and be merry."

"But God said to him, 'You fool! This very night your life will be demanded from you. Then who will get what you have prepared for yourself?'

"This is how it will be with those who store up things for themselves but are not rich toward God" (Luke 12:16-21 TNIV).

And of course, this parallels Jesus's well-known teaching:

Do not store up for yourselves treasures on earth, where moth and rust destroy, and where thieves break in and steal. But store up for yourselves treasures in heaven, where moth and rust do not destroy, and where thieves do not break in and steal. For where your treasure is, there your heart will be also (Matthew 6:19-21 TNIV).

But what do these teachings *mean*? So often, well-worn religion puts its familiar old gloss on them, causing us to mentally check out, thinking that we already know what they mean—and let's face it, we find this standard interpretation pretty well unattainable!

So, what does it mean to be "rich toward God," to "store up for ourselves treasures in heaven"? Again, religion would have us believe that this means we need to join a monastery or cloister somewhere, whiling away our days, pining for the hereafter. But I find that the biblical—and experiential—definition of *Heaven* is so much more radical.

I would like you to try a thought experiment with me. We are going to enact Paul's counsel in Romans 12:2: *"Do not conform any longer to the pattern of this world, but be transformed by the renewing of your mind"*

(NIV). Please pause for a moment and take a mental inventory: What has the "pattern of this world" (which includes the pattern of religion!) taught you about:

- Being rich toward God?

- Eternal life?

- Being in Heaven?

Take about five minutes and consider the conglomeration of what you've been taught, what you've seen on religious programming on television, and what you've told your coworkers or friends or loved ones.

Finished? OK. Now, be present with the following passages of Scripture, letting the *immediacy* of their words wash over you as I emphasize present-tense realities and accomplished facts. Let's start with Jesus's moving prayer in John 17:

> *This **is** eternal life, that they may **know** You, the only true God, and Jesus Christ whom You have sent....Father, I desire that they also, whom You have given Me, **be with Me** where **I am,** so that they may **see** My glory which You have given Me, for You loved Me before the foundation of the world. ...I do not ask on behalf of these alone, but for those also who believe in Me through their word; that they may all **be** one; even as You, Father, **are** in Me and I in You, that they also may **be** in Us.... The glory which You have given Me I **have given** to them, that*

*they may **be one,** just as We **are** one; I in them and You in Me, that they may **be** perfected in unity, so that the world may know that You sent Me, and loved them, even as You have loved Me* (John 17:3, 24, 20-23 NASB, emphasis mine).

*You have not come to a mountain that can be touched…But you **have come** to Mount Zion, to the city of the living God, the heavenly Jerusalem. You **have come** to thousands upon thousands of angels in joyful assembly, to the church of the firstborn, whose names are written in heaven. You **have come** to God, the Judge of all, to the spirits of the righteous made perfect, to Jesus the mediator of a new covenant, and to the sprinkled blood that speaks a better word than the blood of Abel* (Hebrews 12:18a; 22-24 TNIV, emphasis mine).

*Whoever **is** united with the Lord **is** one with Him in spirit* (1 Corinthians 6:17 TNIV).

*God **raised us** up with Christ and **seated** us with Him in the heavenly realms in Christ Jesus* (Ephesians 2:6 NIV, emphasis mine).

Do you see it? Far from being pie-in-the-sky, sweet by-and-by, *Heaven, eternal life,* and even *union with God* are present-tense, right-now realities! Jesus isn't teaching deferment-religion, the kind that Marx called "the opiate of the masses." He's not giving us an "escape-ology theology." No, instead Jesus is asking us to see with a new pair of eyes, one that sees worrying about tomorrow as the dead-end street that it is in light of the incomparable vitality of living united with *I AM* right now!

 ## The future will never arrive. It is unattainable.

What keeps us from immediacy living—in Heaven right now? We are obsessed with the future. We can break this obsession by observing a simple fact: The future will never arrive. It is unattainable. It is another construct of time that limits the way we live today. It is a way to push action or change or thought into another space in time, essentially ignoring it. If you've ever wanted to remodel your bathroom, you can do it next month. Do you want to start saving money for a new car? Start with your next paycheck. In our minds, we imagine these things happening in the future, and it appeases us in the present. But the reality is that the thing is *not happening*. The concept of the future or tomorrow is completely illusory! Tomorrow never comes.

Would you live differently if there were no tomorrow? In the movie *Groundhog Day*[4], the main character, Phil, played by Bill Murray, is stuck living the same day over and over again. The day is always February 2nd, but he is free to choose what he does every time. The circumstances are the same, but his choices and actions are up to him. The main character experiences every emotion possible for such a reality. Once never seeing tomorrow sinks in, he is depressed. He sees no point to living in the now and tries to kill himself numerous ways.

But then, something shifts. Phil decides to put his time to good use and becomes a do-gooder. He changes flat tires for old ladies and takes a homeless man out to lunch and saves a boy from falling out of a tree. He decides to improve himself after a while too. He learns the piano; he learns to ice sculpt. Eventually, he falls in love with a woman he works with each day. After some missteps with romance (in trying to re-create past February 2nds!), he finds solace in learning to live in the now, if that means loving her well and enjoying her presence. It is at this point that time re-starts, with Phil learning to savor each day as it comes.

The changes Phil goes through are humorous, painful, and hopeful. But what makes this film so intriguing is the concept of abandoning tomorrow. What would we live like if today was all we had? Would we abandon fear and worry? Would we care a little less about what other people thought of us? Would we care a little less about our own internal monologues? But, of course, this is silly—isn't it? *Groundhog Day* is only a movie and we expect a tomorrow just like everyone else.

What would we live like if today was all we had?

Sadly, we believe this is true reality. But if we find ourselves inspired to follow the Way of Jesus, we hear the call to live into the deepest truth, which is that we have access to the mind of Christ (see 1 Cor. 2:16). In Christ, the Eternal Present is continuously unfolding. So if we are living with the mind of Christ, then we ought to be thinking in the Eternal Present along with Him! Jesus took ample opportunity to explain this to His followers in a vivid illustration.

"Do not worry about tomorrow, for tomorrow will worry about itself" (Matt. 6:34 NIV). Give no worry to your clothes or your food or all the things that cause you to stress out because they are not anything for God's people to be concerned about. As God's children, we are kept safe within His grasp. We are provided for; we are thought of and tended to just as well as the flowers of the field and the birds of the air (see Matt. 6).

When Jesus taught His apprentices how to pray, knowing full well that it would set precedent for millions of His followers throughout time, He prayed, *"Give us this day our daily bread"* (Matt. 6:11). When it comes down to our basic and immediate needs, God tells us to ask for them in the now and they will be given to us. Because the fact is, He already has given them to us. We just need to be able to see with the mind of Christ the reality of our daily bread before us.

Jesus continues this prayer, "May *Your Kingdom come, Your will be done, on earth as it is in heaven"* (Matt. 6:10 NIV). As we observed in the mind-renewing passages above—Heaven is not some obscure destination, separated by space and time. It is a reality that we're to see intersecting increasingly with the here and now!

Do you believe that we can find God's wisdom everywhere—even in a 1980s pop song? I do. Let's consider Belinda Carlisle's hit anthem[5]:

> In this world we're just beginning
> To understand the miracle of living.
> Baby, I was afraid before,
> But I'm not afraid anymore.
> Ooh, baby, do you know what that's worth?
> Ooh, Heaven is a place on earth.
> They say in Heaven love comes first—
> We'll make Heaven a place on earth.

Ooh, baby! That's some truth right there! Perfect love casts out all fear, and perfect love is found in the present moment—it's found when we metastasize Jesus's prayer with our very lives, reflecting the Kingdom of Heaven as a place on Earth now. But how do we bring this down to Earth?

Take a moment to stop and think about what is in your mind right now. Are you thinking about what you will eat for dinner? Perhaps you are trying to decide when to take your car in for its oil change. Maybe you are thinking about how you should be exercising right now instead of reading so that you can lose those 10 pounds before you go on vacation next month.

 If the past is dead to us, then the future is never alive to us because life exists only in the now.

All of this is conjecture and hope at best, but worry and distrust at worst. We can call it whatever we like, but the fact remains that the future is something we need to release from our minds. If the past is dead to us, then the future is never alive to us because life exists only in the now.

How we release our minds from worry of the future may seem more difficult than forgetting the past, but it is possible when we learn to live in the Now.

Questions to Ponder

Are you building barns? What are you storing up today in your life? What material things do you value? Why do you value them? _____

_____

_____

_____

In the Lord's Prayer, we ask for our daily bread. What is your daily bread? Do you ask Him for it? If not, why not? _____

_____

_____

What are you worried about right now? If tomorrow did not come, would you still be worried? _____

_____

_____

_____

Paul tells us we have the mind of Christ. If so, what is Christ thinking? How does this change your thinking patterns? _____

_____

_____

Jesus Himself prayed for His daily bread from the Father. What was His daily bread? Are you sharing the same bread? _____

_____

_____

Living in the I AM
Exercise Four: Surrender

Jesus said something that I've always loved, *"Not as the world gives do I give"* (John 14:27b NASB). What's so interesting about this saying is that giving and receiving are such a part of the fabric of the universe if we really look at it. Everything we love, each item we possess, from food to houses, are all just subtle shifts in how we interact with the universe. The difference between having nothing and having something grand is actually very little, when you think of it from a physical sense.

For instance let's say two gentleman happen to both be holding a crumpled up and dirty piece of paper. They appear to be in very similar situations, don't they? And in truth they are. There's very little difference between the two. However, one crumpled piece of paper happens to be a hundred-dollar bill and the other is just an old candy wrapper. What's the difference? There's not one, save the value we have assigned to one and not the other. In a sense Paul knew this when he said he knows how to be abased and how to abound (see Phil. 4:12). Emptiness and fullness are just different sides of the same state of being, if you're living in the Now.

One famous Eastern guru who owned nothing but a blanket (occasionally giving that away) said, "Why give me money? All the money in the universe is mine." He was saying that at the core level we own nothing and we own everything.

Consider the last time you gave something. I know that often there's a feeling we attach to it that says, "This is my thing I'm giving to you. And I hope you understand what a generous gift this is." Rather than giving from a space of compassion and spontaneous openness, it is most easy to give with a thousand golden strings attached. In the end, how we give underlines how we approach the world around us. It is often an extension of our worldview. When we are operating from a place of openness and unconditional love where we sense our oneness with Christ, and indeed all the universe, then we are able to simply be conduits. We recognize that we are not the giver and we are not the receiver; we are simply the channel for God's love.

This is why it's important to cultivate the exercise of giving and learning to receive. As we open our hands to give and receive, in essence we are opening our spirits as well.

Consider choosing two of the exercises below—allow one to be something that you might do on a normal basis, but consciously choose another that would be difficult. Reflect on the difference of these experiences. Remember, the point is not to "get it right," but rather to bring yourself into a place of awareness of what is happening in the now.

Giving Exercises

1. Remember John the Baptist's words: *"If you have two coats, give one away"* (Luke 3:11 MSG). Give away possessions that you have multiples of.

2. Give away something that is valuable to you; then give away something you really don't value at all.

3. If someone compliments you on a possession, give it to them.

4. Make a gift for someone else.

5. Give something to a stranger; then give something to someone you don't like.

6. Give something to a child.

7. Give your ear to someone. Invite someone to tell you their story or whatever is on their heart.

8. Go and sell all you have and give it to the poor (except this book)!

9. Give something to someone, but don't let them know who did it.

10. Find a way to repay your parents for giving you life.

Receiving Exercises

1. Reflect on all the things you've been gifted with in the last month. Try to pay specific attention to how you reacted to these.

2. The next time someone gives you something, don't thank them. (In Hindi there isn't even a word for "thank you." In India, giving is simply a part of your duty. The attitude of the giver is, "Why should I be thanked for what I am compelled to do?")

3. For a day, eat only the things that others offer to you. The trick to this is that you cannot tell someone this is what you're doing.

4. If you experience a need, choose to exclusively take it to God. Don't talk about it with anyone else. And don't attempt to fill the need yourself by asking for assistance.

CHAPTER FOUR

Now!

Practicing the presence of God is not on trial. Countless saints have already proved it. Indeed, the spiritual giants of all ages have known it. The results of this effort begin to show clearly in a month. They grow rich after six months, and glorious after ten years. This is the secret of the great saints of all ages. "Pray without ceasing," said Paul, "in everything make your wants known unto God." "As many as are led by the spirit of God, these are the sons of God."

—Frank Laubach[1]

There is not in the world a kind of life more sweet and delightful, than that of a continual

conversation with God; those only can comprehend it who practice and experience it.
—Brother Lawrence[2]

How often is the word *now* used in Scripture to start a story, explain God's actions, or salted into Jesus's teachings? In the NIV translation the word *now* is used 1,192 times. The King James Version uses it 1,321 times, and the New American Standard—often considered the most word-for-word accurate translation—uses *now* a whopping 2,166 times!

- *Now* there was a famine in the land....

- *Now* when Jesus saw great multitudes...

- *Now* the earth was formless and empty....

- *Now* one of the Pharisees invited Jesus....

(See Genesis 26:1 NIV; Matthew 8:18; Genesis 1:2 NIV; Luke 7:36 NIV.)

God's positive actions are still offered in the future, but the *blessing* is only offered in the here and now.

Now can be a manner of speech, but could it also imply a type of living, thinking, or speaking that recognizes *the Now* as the only potent moment? Early in Jesus's ministry, He spoke the famous words that were recorded as the beatitudes. *"Blessed are you who hunger now, for you will be satisfied. Blessed are you who weep now, for you will laugh"* (Luke 6:21 NIV). Positive action still is offered in the future, but the blessing is offered only in the Now. That needs to be said again. *God's positive actions are still offered in the future, but the* **blessing** *is only offered in the here and now.*

I've referenced Abraham before as someone who was called out of the past and into the Now. His story is mentioned all over Scripture, reminding us of his exceptional faith, his trust in I AM, that birthed an entire nation. When we first meet Abraham in the Hebrew Bible, God asks him to leave his homeland and go to a land He will show him. God doesn't tell him where or when or why, but He promises blessing. For the next several decades, Abraham and his family travel all over Canaan, Egypt, Bethel, Sodom, and the land of the Philistines. Finally, 25 years after the promise, Abraham received a son. At last God proved good on His promise and delivered the blessing Abraham had so longed for.

That is, until God tested Abraham. God called out:

> *"Abraham!" And* [Abraham] *said,* **"Here I am**.*"* [God] *said, "Take now your son, your only son, whom you love, Isaac, and go to the land of Moriah, and offer him there as a burnt offering on one of the mountains of which I will tell you"* (Genesis 22:1-2 NASB).

But how could God have promised Abraham a son only to take him away? Had God changed His mind, or did He contradict Himself? These are the questions I would have had in my mind. I would have wanted to let God know that I was counting on a future I'd envisioned. I would make sure He understands the importance of my plans and my dreams of future generations. I would remind God of His past promises.

Amazingly enough, Abraham followed through on the Lord's request and took his son up a mountain to sacrifice him there. He built the altar, gathered the wood, and tied his son to it all. This is such a symbolic moment. The altar is, in many ways, a memorial to what *has* been. The altar always represents a remembering of what was. Now here, flayed out upon that symbol of the past, we see the child of the promise—the future. This is a complete picture of past and future laid bare before God. And one can only imagine the horror and pain of that moment or what Abraham was thinking when he took out the knife to slay his son and all that he represented.

But thank God for Genesis 22:11-12:

But the angel of the LORD *called to him from heaven and said, "Abraham, Abraham!" And he said, "Here I am." He said, "Do not stretch out your hand against the lad, and do nothing to him; for **now** I know that you fear God, since*

*you have not withheld your son, your only son,
from Me"* (NASB, emphasis mine).

Two things need emphasizing in this story: the crucial qualifier of *now* and the present-reality of divine availability that Abraham dared to live in. The way religion tends to tell this story is either that God always meant to spare Isaac, or else that God changed His mind. What if there's a provocative third possibility?

What if God did *not* change His mind? God asked Abraham to *"take now"* his son to sacrifice him. All He was asking of Abraham was to act in the Now, to follow through on only what he was told. At the moment of climax, God intervenes with what we can only imagine to be a shout. "Don't lay a hand on your son. *Now* I know how much you fear God because of your obedience to Me." In the Now, God spares Isaac's life and Abraham's heart. In the Now, God directs Abraham. This is how God can say two seemingly different things and they are still true. In the Now, God tests us and blesses us. In the Now, we are free to choose obedience or rebellion.

This reading of the beautiful story of the sacrifice of Isaac reminds me of one of the great prayer warriors of our age, Rosalind Rinker.[3] Ros was a lovely woman who was a missionary in the early 20th century. She experienced a frustration in her prayer life for years. What was that frustration? In many ways it may be what countless of us have experienced. An endless series of prayers and petitions only to receive no response or to feel like nothing has been accomplished. It seemed like her prayers were ineffective.

Then suddenly she felt as if God whispered His solution to her one day. It came in the form of a crisis, as it so often happens. At the Chinese mission there was a young girl who needed healing, desperately. Ros, instead of praying a large and grandiose prayer, simply asked God to let her know the next step. Instinctively she felt that she should go get a certain medicine. When she arrived at the doctor and procured the medicine she then felt prompted to ask God to show her the next step again. This occurred several times, until finally, in a miraculous turn of events, the child recovered. From then on, Ros committed to the task of only asking God for the next step. Time and time again, this proved to be exactly how God worked in her life and hundreds of thousands of others. God is always calling people to live into this present work. Nothing more. Just one step at a time.

The second emphasis in this story is the response of the father of the great monotheistic faiths, which we now name "Abrahamic"—Judaism, Christianity, and Islam. This man, who has inspired nearly two-thirds of the world spiritually, had a simple attitude toward life:

"Here I am."

How closely it echoes the voice of God reverberating before creation—*I AM!* We are told that Abraham was justified by faith and it was *"credited to him as righteousness"* (Gal. 3:6; Rom. 4:3; James 2:23 NIV). We are implored to be like Abraham.

And yet, when religion teaches us about "here I am," it invariably goes to willpower. The altar call is shouting to your soul. The Great Commission weighing on your heart. *Here I am, Lord. Send me to Africa…!*

But what if the phrase has less to do with will and much more to do with being? The statement "Here I am" can stand as a declaration of presence rather than offering alone. God calls Abraham to faith in the now and Abraham responds with "Here I am!" in the same breath.

 The statement "Here I am" can stand as a declaration of presence rather than offering alone.

Another example of God's Eternal Present is shown to us in Deuteronomy. God has fulfilled His promise to Abraham; the nation of Israel is a homeless people wandering the desert after escaping Egypt's captivity. Here God desires to shepherd His people into greater trust, obedience, and hope.

> *Now what I am commanding you **today**…See, I set before you **today** life and prosperity, death and destruction. For I command you **today**….*

> *I declare to you **this day*** (Deuteronomy 30:11,
> 15-16, 18 NIV, emphasis mine).

Is God emphasizing a certain day? Do you think He is being unclear about His timeline? Or is He just bringing life to the present moment because He is there, because He is speaking? It is the present-moment immediacy of God's intimacy and guidance, as much as it is the particular commands, that were so precious to the ancient Israelites.

The New Testament is peppered with an emphasis on the present as well. In Romans 4, Paul is still pointing us to Abraham's example. Abraham received God's promise of blessing and presence before he was even circumcised to show that the promise was given because of faith—trust in I AM—alone, and not anything else.

> *As it is written: "I have made you a father of many nations." He is our father in the sight of God, in whom he believed—**the God who gives life to the dead and calls things that are not as though they were*** (Romans 4:17 NIV, emphasis mine).

This last phrase can also be translated as God, *"who... calls into being that which does not exist"* (NASB).

We call Abraham "father" not because he got God's attention by living like a saint, but because God made something out of Abraham when he was a nobody. Isn't that what we've always read in Scripture,

God saying to Abraham, "I set you up as father of many peoples"? Abraham was first named "father" and then became a father because he dared to trust God to do what only God could do: raise the dead to life, with a word make something out of nothing. When everything was hopeless, Abraham believed anyway, deciding to live not on the basis of what he saw he couldn't do, but on what God said he would do. And so he was made father of a multitude of peoples. God Himself said to him, *"You're going to have a big family, Abraham!"* (Rom. 4:17-18 MSG).

God spoke to Abram and called him by his "true name": Abraham. He did not speak to him as a washed-up old man or a leader in the making. He spoke to him as though Abraham were who he was meant to be. God called Abraham by his real name. If God sees you a certain way, then so be it.

If Abraham's example is not enough for us, Paul writes this image in bigger and bigger terms:

> *You show that you are a letter from Christ, the result of our ministry, written not with ink but with the Spirit of the living God, not on tablets of stone but on tablets of human hearts.*

> *Such confidence as this is ours through Christ before God. Not that we are competent in our-selves to claim anything for ourselves, but our competence comes from God. He has made us competent as ministers of a new covenant—not*

of the letter but of the Spirit; for the letter kills, but the Spirit gives life (2 Corinthians 3:3-6 NIV).

Our ministry, our message, our life is dwelling within us in this very moment. We are vessels of life-giving.

Paul tells us that we are living letters—walking, breathing, blood-pumping Life Letters. We have not written on ourselves. We don't have the Eternal Ink on our own, yet Christ has been our message, our text, our pen and ink. All our confidence and competence is in Him. Therefore, we live and move and interact with the world with a confidence that cannot be shaken. Our ministry, our message, our life is dwelling within us in this very moment. We are vessels of life-giving.

Sometimes I don't feel like much of a "life-giving vessel." In fact, I can feel pretty low at times. As soon as I begin to look at the past, with its regrets or remembrances, or the future, with my anticipations and expectations, my anxieties and my aspirations, I get turned around. But then, along with the prophets and apostles, I say, "Here I am." Simple, without reservation, I offer myself—just as I am, without a plea, in this moment. "Lord, take me—take my past, and take even the future with all of its God-given promises. Take it all, free me from the prison of time—to live in Your eternal today." In that moment, everything changes.

Questions to Ponder

As Abraham was promised Isaac and then challenged to sacrifice him, God seemed to be contradicting Himself. Have you felt God's contradictions in your own life? _____

_____

_____

Though He may be asking for your most precious thing, are you able to say, "Here I am?" _____

_____

_____

What name has God given you? Do you know it yet? Have you asked for it? _____

_____

_____

We are Life Letters. What kind of letter are you writing? If your friends and family are reading you, what do they see? _____

_____

_____

What is the "next step" right now? _____

_____

_____

⚬∞⚬

Living in the I AM
Exercise Five: Awareness

The goal of awareness isn't enlightenment; it's the state of being aware. In the next several exercises, don't try for any great revelation or bells and whistles. Preferably, don't try for anything at all! The point is to observe. Sit back and take it all in. See all the sights. Witness everything. Consider how your hands get sweaty or how your back aches as you sit still. Be aware of the ideas that float across your consciousness—how this may seem like a waste of time, how you might be bored, how you didn't get to sleep in this morning, and so forth. Allow yourself to view *you* through the witness of the Spirit—mind, body, and soul.

The following exercise is specifically designed to get people to "lose their minds and find their senses," as the famous psychologist Fritz Perls was fond of saying. As we've said earlier, too many of us live in our heads. We mainly think and fantasize and imagine and conjecture and worry and stress and construct whole empires in theory! We spend very little time being aware of what our actual sensations in any given moment are. This boils down to an inability to live in the present moment, the I AM of God. We are so rarely in the Now and so frequently in the past, with its regrets and mistakes, or in the future, with its anticipations or anxieties. While I believe we must learn from the past and plan sufficiently for the future, I believe that contact with God is always in the here and now. "To succeed in prayer it is essential to develop the ability to make contact with the present and to stay there."[4] In the end, the best way to come into the sacredness of now is to evacuate the inner sanctum of our thought life through coming to grips with the sensations of the body.

Body Exercise

Get comfortable. Close your eyes. In these next few minutes, attempt to feel as many sensations in your body as you can, even though (and perhaps especially because) you aren't normally aware of them. Sense how your body feels right now. Take note of the aches and pains, of the soreness or the tension. Now become aware of how your clothes feel against your body. Notice the sensation of the fabric on your skin, how it ripples and flows. Does it tingle? Do you feel it all? Next, let yourself become aware of your feet. How are they positioned? Do they feel cramped or crowded or crushed? If you're wearing shoes or socks, how do they feel against the skin of your feet? Now become especially observant of how you're seated. What kind of posture do you have? Are your shoulders slouching? Are you upright? Feel the tug of gravity in your body pushing it downward toward the floor.

Then begin at the top of your head; allow yourself to feel the way your hair falls there. Next, your facial muscles. Become fully aware of your mouth, your ears, your chin. Continue down your body to your shoulders. Explicitly note what they are doing and how they feel. Apply all of your consciousness to your right arm, then to your left, then on to your hands and into your fingers. Travel farther down the length of your person. Your back…your thighs…your feet…your toes…. Repeat this whole exercise several times.

During this, truly allow yourself to *feel* the sensations of the body. Don't just imagine what they might be like. Actually go there. Inhabit your neck, the soft of your arms, your stomach, your calf and ankles, then move on to another part of the body. Do this for several minutes, remembering that the goal is not to "succeed" or have some "deep" experience, but rather to acknowledge what is occurring in you—true awareness.

CHAPTER FIVE

Faith for the Now: Knowing God

Experiencing the present purely is being emptied and hollow: you catch grace as a man fills his cup under a waterfall.

—Annie Dillard[1]

Become at ease with the state of "not knowing." This takes you beyond mind because the mind is always trying to conclude and interpret. It is afraid of not knowing. So, when you can be at ease with not knowing, you have already gone beyond the mind. A deeper knowing that is non-conceptual then arises out of that state.

—Eckhart Tolle[2]

When we fall into thinking the word "God" is the thing, we become idol worshippers, worshipping idols made not of wood but by the mind. Mental idols.

—J. Francis Stroud[3]

The glorious riches of this mystery, which is Christ in you, the hope of glory

—Colossians 1:27 NIV

Life is only alive in the Now. You can't be alive yesterday. You can't be alive tomorrow. The moment you are standing in is the only moment that really exists. *Now* is the precise place where every form of calling and creativity comes from. Now is the specific spot where we are invited to become participants with the very life of God. But this is a tremendously difficult concept for most of us to accept. Why? Because before we understand the power that is *the Now*, we have to understand the God who *is*.

There are two great dangers in our approach to the Most High. The first is to imagine God as unknowable and removed from our lives. By doing this we relegate the God of Abraham, Isaac, and Jacob to the infinitely impersonal role of being just a force, incapable of relating to our highly personal realities. The second danger is, paradoxically, to entertain the thought that God— who dwells in *"unapproachable light"* that no one may enter (1 Tim. 6:16 NIV)—can be grasped. I realize that these two statements are contradictions. But both are equally true in our faith journey.

On one hand we have to realize that God is *for* us and seems to process Himself into the whole of the cosmos simply to whisper to us of His deep affection. This is the God of miracles who is mighty to save. This is the God who parts seas, is poured out upon His sons and daughters, and fills us with His presence. This is the God of a thousand names, each one naming a different aspect of His person:

- El Shaddai—the All-Sufficient Provider

- Elohim—the one who preserves

- Jehovah-Ropha—the one who heals

- Jehovah-Nissi—the Lord, our Banner

- Jehovah-Shammah—the Lord who is there (present)

The roll call of the divine is eternal and attests to God's hyper-abundance in our lives.

There's a lovely little story about a young guppy who swims over to an elder in his particular school of fish and asks where the ocean is. The wise fish, with laughter in his eyes, said that the ocean was all around—they were surrounded by the ocean. For a moment the young guppy paused then shook his head and said, "This?" pointing to their surroundings. "This is no ocean. This is just water!" And he went away to continue his search for the ocean.

Stop looking, little fish! The ocean envelops you, holds you, and nourishes you. Just because you fail to understand it, identify it, or explore all of it does not mean it is elsewhere. Just like the ocean, God is here, now, and infinitely accessible. In our search for receiving a clearer picture of God, the first step is to realize that there's no great secret. The question of discovering God shifts from wondering where He might be, to asking where *isn't* He? If our Lord is in all things, where will we *not* find Him?

On the other hand we must acknowledge that if God is really who we believe Him to be—infinite—then God is infinitely beyond our ability to conceive of Him. Because we are creatures and not the Creator, because our words are endlessly boring shells that only hint at what we're actually trying to describe, we have to acknowledge that at our best we can't articulate the ultimate grandeur of I AM.

There's really so little we can know, so little we can grasp of God in just one lifetime. The saint and theologian Thomas Aquinas spent years writing countless pages about how we may know God, then at the end of his life he concludes with this: "We remain joined to Him as to one unknown."[4] Similarly the apostle Paul writes in one of his last letters, as an aged believer, "Oh that I might know Him..." (see Phil. 3:10), as if to say that in the pursuit of God he is still a seeker, still a new-born in the blossoming awareness of the Holy. Paul and Aquinas are both acknowledging that the surface of God can't be scratched. God is endless in every direction, and just when we believe that He has been figured out, we have missed the point altogether.

One might read those two very different thoughts and think that there's just no hope! But the truth—reality—lies in the dynamic tension created between these two oppositional certainties. While the mind cannot bridge the gap between these oppositional realities, the heart can. God is impossible to have "figured out," but is easy to love.

 God is impossible to have "figured out," but is easy to love.

We love God, and manifest the joy that God's love brings, when we live in the Now. Paul consistently spoke of this tension of knowing and not knowing God. He prayed for the church in Ephesus:

> *...And I pray that you, being rooted and established in love, may have power, together with all the saints, to grasp how wide and long and high and deep is the love of Christ, and to know this love that surpasses knowledge—that you may be filled to the measure of all the fullness of God.*

Now to Him who is able to do immeasurably more than all we ask or imagine, according to His power that is at work within us (Ephesians 3:17-20 NIV).

Yet it is as though Paul happily throws up his hands in defeat when he cries, *"Oh, the depth of the riches of the wisdom and knowledge of God! How unsearchable His judgments, and His paths beyond tracing out"* (Rom. 11:33 NIV).

We long to know Christ in God and understand Him completely. But perhaps the better longing to nourish is our longing to understand His love. It is unsearchable and endless, yet we pray to know it to its full heights and depths.

Right now you may be a guppy in an ocean. The mystery of God may be everywhere around you. Who is this God whom we know *now*? It is to this question—what some sages say is the *only* question—that we now turn our attention.

Questions to Ponder

It's true that God has more names than we know. In this chapter, several of His names are listed. Which ones are most precious to you right now? Have you been referring to God by His specific names? _____

_____

_____

_____

Have you "figured" God out? What do you know of Him? _____

_____

_____

Are there things of Him that you do not understand? What concepts or questions push you to the edge of your understanding? Is it possible for you to be grateful for these limits? _____

_____

_____

Living in the I AM
Exercise Six: Praise

Not all that long ago I met a rabbi who openly informed me that he rarely thanked God for his food. He commented that he had no clue if it would actually be nourishing, tasty, or adequate to meet his needs, so why should he bother being thankful for it until he knew. I was alarmed, just as you probably are. It seems so ungrateful a stance, bringing back a memory of my grandfather suggesting I not "look a gift horse in the mouth." If everything is a gift, then be thankful, no matter how small. And of course that is how most of us believe.

However, in many ways I wonder if we're not all that different from the gentleman I just described. We wait to see how everything turns out. We conveniently become very grateful for the things we enjoy. In truth, this attitude shuts the windows of Heaven and effectively cuts us off from the Now. In order to fully bring the strands of God's glorious future into the present, we must adopt a posture of praise.

God is worthy of our attention and praise, but giving Him our adoration actually does something good for us. The reality of our praising declares us to be fully alive, responding to a Being we love and adore. While there are many types of prayer, I believe that this one most defines the life of the believer whose heart is open toward God. The prayer of praise is based on the belief that every gift (literally everything) comes from God and is good and perfect (see James 1:17). Nothing happens in our lives that sends God into a panic. He is not seated on the edge of His throne biting His fingernails about what's happening. Everything happens by God, through God, for God, and of God. Everything. Can you even imagine?

If this is true—if God is *this* big—then there isn't really anything that God cannot be praised for. In fact the act of praising God for everything, including tragedy and the things that have yet to come, enables us to accept reality as it is and also take leaps of faith or risks because we begin to understand that all things work together for good (see Rom. 8:28).

Praise Exercise 1

Think of something either historic or current that you are frustrated by, something that is distressing, or something that you feel a sense of guilt over. If you have any sort of complicity or blame for this then certainly confess that to God and express your sorrow. Now, having done that—*praise God* for it. Describe (or perhaps mouth the words) how you understand that even *this* works together for your good and His glory. In this way you are fulfilling the command that we are given through Paul: *"Be joyful always; pray continually; give thanks in all circumstances…"* (1 Thess. 5:16-18 NIV).

Praise Exercise 2

Begin your prayers to God with praise. In fact, make it a habit of praising God simply for who He is, regardless of what you feel in this moment. Take care to think on His character, His feelings, His promises, His actions. Remember, He is a Being who interacts with humanity. Try not to think about yourself or your own situations, but put your attention on God.

CHAPTER SIX

I AM Is All in All

Souls wherein the Spirit dwells, illuminated by the Spirit, themselves become spiritual, and send forth their grace to others. Hence comes...abiding in God, the being made like to God, and, highest of all, the being made God.

—St. Basil the Great[1]

The Only-begotten Son of God, wanting us to be partakers of his divinity, assumed our human nature so that, having become man, he might make men gods.

—St. Thomas Aquinas[2]

The Word became flesh and the Son of God became the Son of Man: so that man, by entering into communion with the Word and thus receiving divine sonship, might become a son of God

—St. Irenaeus[3]

God became man, so that man might become God.

—Athanasius[4]

Morality is indispensable: but the Divine Life, which gives itself to us and which calls us to be gods, intends for us something in which morality will be swallowed up. We are to be remade... we shall find underneath it all a thing we have never yet imagined: a real man, an ageless god, a son of God, strong, radiant, wise, beautiful, and drenched in joy.

—C.S. Lewis[5]

You are not a human being having a spiritual experience—you are a spiritual being having a human experience.

—Wayne Dyer[6]

J.B. Phillips, a celebrated Bible translator, rocked the spiritual landscape in 1961 with the publication of his power-packed little book, *Your God Is Too Small.*[7] What a revelation loaded into just the title! I am constantly reading books that enlarge my mind and prepare my heart to receive further revelation into the height, depth, mercy, and expansiveness of our God. I've noticed that some titles themselves seem to carry an anointing: *The Practice of the Presence of God*[8] and *The Sacrament of the Present Moment*[9] in centuries past, to *God Chasers*[10] today. This hunger is paralleled in the strong (albeit controversial) impact such contemporary titles as *The Power of Now*[11] and *The Secret*[12] have had in the past few years.

 When we speak, we can unleash the very oracles of God into the Earth.

"Death and life are in the power of the tongue" (Prov. 18:21); this is true of the written word as well. *"The Word was made flesh"* (John 1:14). Seamlessly, we are living correspondence from the living God, the author of our faith. When we speak, we can unleash the very oracles of God into the Earth—words from God that don't return void, but accomplish everything that God has planted in our hearts. (For some rich Scripture meditation in this, see Second Corinthians 3:2-3, First Peter 4:11, Hebrews 12:2, and Isaiah 55:11.)

How can opening ourselves to the present moment yield our human spirits even more to God's divine authorship living and speaking through us to reap abundant life? Let's go straight to God's Word itself to see how "our" God is, indeed, too small!

A Radical Proposal

When you begin to see the Holy Spirit shimmering in each moment as it unfolds, you begin to develop *divine boundary issues*. In other words, you start wondering where God ends and everything else—you, me, and creation—begins. Is this blasphemy? To the chains of religion, maybe, but the testimony of Scripture reveals a *much bigger* God. *"...You give life to all..."* (Neh. 9:6 NASB).

As we come to this realization, perhaps we will be like Jacob, who exclaims after wrestling with God, *"God was in this place—and I, I did not know"* (Gen. 28:16, Rabbi Lawrence Kushner translation).

It is not as if we are God. No, we must be clear on that point. God is eternal Creator and we are temporal creatures. We are emanations; God is our source. But a valuable theology recognizes the unscaleability of God. He will not be measured or boxed in by our ideas. He will not end where we tell Him to or start where we think He does. God is *God,* and He is everywhere.

For instance: How many times have you heard it said that hell is "eternal separation from God"? Yet the Psalmist, who expresses I AM's ever-presence, even in the midst of our deepest suffering, has a different understanding:

> *O Lord, You have searched me and known me.*
> *You know my sitting down and my rising up;*

You understand my thought afar off.
You comprehend my path and my lying down,
And are acquainted with all my ways.
For there is not a word on my tongue,
But behold, O LORD, You know it altogether.
You have hedged me behind and before,
And laid Your hand upon me.
Such knowledge is too wonderful for me;
It is high, I cannot attain it.
Where can I go from Your Spirit?
Or where can I flee from Your presence?
If I ascend into heaven, You are there;
If I make my bed in hell, behold, You are there.
If I take the wings of the morning,
And dwell in the uttermost parts of the sea,
Even there Your hand shall lead me,
And Your right hand shall hold me.
If I say, "Surely the darkness shall fall on me,"
Even the night shall be light about me;
Indeed, the darkness shall not hide from You,
But the night shines as the day;
The darkness and the light are both alike to You
(Psalm 139:1-12 NKJV).

I read this Psalm and I infer that God is everywhere, but even more powerful and touching to me is the idea that there is nowhere I can be or go where He will not be or go. He wants to be with us, in us. It is His choosing that we would be unified.

We may struggle to understand if God is in hell then. But more importantly, is there somewhere that God can't go? Won't go? When Jesus was crucified and placed in the tomb, He was not exactly stuck in one place. The walls of stone and earth were not limiting His life. Instead, He was busy going places. In the Apostle's Creed, it states that He "descended into hell" where He proclaimed victory over death and then ascended into Heaven where He sat at the right hand of God. As soon as He paid the price of reconciliation, He was quick to spread the word. There was nowhere He would not go for us.

Is God somehow in everything? I've concluded that this is what Scripture teaches. And yet, God is still one Being. Confusing? It is a paradox to be sure. We may believe in the triune nature of God, yet we believe Him to be one being. This has been the way of Christianity and the way of God's children for centuries.

The confession of God's oneness begins with Israel's most sacred confession, the Shema: "Listen, Israel, YHWH is God; YHWH is one."

What do you suppose this means? That there is only one real and living God? Certainly. But what if it means so much more than this? Venerable rabbis offer us intriguing insight on this:

> "When we say 'the Lord is One,' we mean that nothing other than God exists in all the universe."
>
> —Rabbi Baal Shem Tov

"The meaning of 'YHVH is One' is not that He is the only God negating other gods, but… there is no being other than Him, even though it seems otherwise to most people."
—Rabbi Sfat Emet[13]

 But if there was nothing outside of God when creation was birthed, out of what are we made?

Could this be? From the perspective of time, God is our Creator and we are His creatures. But if there was nothing outside of God when creation was birthed, out of what are we made? From the perspective of the Now, is it possible that we are all emanations of the Almighty? Two more passages from Deuteronomy shine some light on this:

For you were shown, to know it, that YHWH is the God; there is nothing else beside Him (Deuteronomy 4:35).

Know this day, and lay it on your heart, that YHWH is God in heaven above and on the earth beneath; there is none else (Deuteronomy 4:39).[14]

Nothing else! Could it be, from the perspective of the eternal present moment, that we are completely enveloped in God's intimacy, presence, and care—to the point that the very concept of independent *existence* is a mistaken view of reality? Religion is quick to tout the *sovereignty* of God—God's true and biblical Lordship over all reality—but they fall short of the full biblical revelation of Christ as the All in All. And yet if we listen to the prophetic word God spoke to Isaiah, can we really conclude anything else?

> *I am the* LORD, *and there is none else, there is no God beside Me...* (Isaiah 45:5).

May we open our eyes to the *Now* and receive this truth.

Nested Within God

Jay Michaelson, a contemporary Jewish author and spiritual seeker, has written a book that examines this vision of God in depth. In his book, *Everything Is God: The Radical Path of Nondual Judaism*, Michaelson theorizes the unity of all things based upon a true knowing of God. I might not agree with every word in this book, but there are many points where he teaches on the Hebrew Bible (Old Testament) that resonate with my spirit. All truth is God's truth, amen? The apostle Paul was emboldened to see divine revelation in the "unauthorized" (pagan) poetry of his day when he recognized that *"in Him we live, and move, and have our being"* (Acts 17:28). He didn't shy away from truth because of its source—because Paul knew, ultimately, that there is but one source for all truth. In this same spirit of humility and discernment, let's look at what Michaelson has to say. He writes:

> If God is infinite, God is all there really is. If we suppose that a physical object is just that object and not God, we have supposed limit in the limitless, which is a contradiction. If the object has its own separate existence, then God exists everywhere but suddenly stops at the border of the object; it is thus not God. This of course cannot be if God is infinite; therefore, the object must be filled with God. Whatever its form, the substance is Divine. Likewise, even the "self" is a phenomenon which, like a rainbow, appears only from a certain perspective. If God is infinite, then by necessity, God is reading these words, writing them, and dwelling within them. Who else could you possibly be?[15]

The question is: How far are we willing to take *"I and the Father are One...as we are, Father, let them be too—one with Us and each other"* (see John 10:30; John 17:21a NIV)? What does it look like to believe that *"in Him we live and move and have our being"* (Acts 17:28 NIV)? How do we behave if we believe that *the one who joins with the Lord is one spirit with God?* (See 1 Corinthians 6:17.)

We are joined in God, and yet, we are still just us.

Now, before this sounds too much like New Age heresy, Michaelson reins it in by telling us:

> Even if you are God, you are not the master of the universe. Sorry. On the relative level, you are still you. On an absolute level, however, the phenomenon of "you" is something that happens to God, and the temporary agglomeration of consciousness and matter which you are is like a ripple on a pond.[16]

In other words, we are joined in God, and yet, we are still just us.

In Western spiritual traditions, God is seen as one Being, while reality—that is, you, me, cats, and trees—have their own real and distinct identities. Eastern traditions tend to stress the idea of *monism*—that all reality is one—but very often "God" can be manifest in any number of forms. Variations of this are known as the philosophical problem of "the one and the many." Jesus says that true worshipers will worship God in Spirit and in truth (see John 4:23)—in other words, we will accept any truth, revealed in any culture or hemisphere, that the Spirit opens our eyes to.

This is what I'm seeing right now: Though these ideas of the one and the many seem to conflict with one another in the natural realm, in the Spirit realm a Trinity-shaped spiritual experience seeks to answer them both. The genius of God's revelation in Christ is that God enfolds reality: God is the One, manifesting creation as the many. That is, God is both one God and plural in community with Himself—Father, Son, and Spirit. Both are true—both are real.

And similarly, we—humanity, creation, the "third heaven" realm, everything—are *one* from a vital and important perspective. Even from a physics perspective! The idea that I am a discrete being and you are a discrete being and that my chair is a discrete entity is an *effect* from a particular vantage point. But on a molecular level, I, my chair, you, soil, stars—we're all very permeable, all in motion; we're more *patterns* than discrete objects. And the patterns eventually change, fade, and are reborn. This is why the DJ Moby sings: "We are all made of stars." The poets were right. It's true!

Let's talk about *holons* for a moment. There is a philosopher named Ken Wilber who has popularized the term. *Holons* are "Wholes that are also parts."[17] We are all whole-parts—a discrete entity in and of ourselves, but a vital part of something else. For example, our heart is "a heart," but it is also part of a vast blood-delivery system in our bodies. I am me, but I'm also a vital part of my family. On a larger scale, I am a part of a community and nation and planet and solar system. From a God's-eye view, everything created is one giant eco-system, one giant Body. And ultimately, this eco-system is a holon nested within God.

Just as light is both particle and wave, so too are we all one in God—and yet everything also has its own unique identity, including (especially!) God.

Both of these facets of reality give glory to God and a sense of wonder to life. At this moment in the West, we stress dualism too much, endlessly trying to figure out right from wrong, good from evil. We might think that this is what being spiritual is all about, but Scripture names this as the fruit of the Knowledge of Good and Evil! Real discernment comes from the Spirit of God residing within us; us frantically trying to figure such things out is a fruit of the flesh. We don't want Western dualism any more than we want Eastern undifferentiated monism. Balance is needed. Perfect balance is found when we flow with Holy Spirit in the Now.

This was the animating passion of the apostle Paul as he brought the Good News to religious people and an empire built on violence, greed, and segregation. Our oneness with God in Christ was Paul's antidote to racism, sexism, and classism, as evidenced in his iconic words to the faith community in Galatia:

> *There is neither Jew nor Greek, slave nor free, male nor female, for you are all one in Christ Jesus* (Galatians 3:28 NIV).

Lest we're tempted to put limitations on *who* is invited into this circle of care and reconciliation of former enemies, Paul brings this same theme in even sharper relief in a later letter to another church:

> *Here there is no Greek or Jew, circumcised or uncircumcised, barbarian, Scythian, slave or free, but Christ is all, and is in all* (Colossians 3:11 NIV).

After His resurrection and ascension, where is Christ? *All* in all! Christ doesn't get any bigger than that, praise God!

Let's get radical for a moment—how far are we willing to take this revelation of God in all things? "Do not look at a stone and say, 'that is a stone and not God,'" wrote a venerable sixteenth-century rabbi, Moses Cordovero. "For you have dualized—God forbid. Instead, know that the stone is a thing pervaded by Divinity."[18] Don't dualize: What God has joined together in the love of His Son—you, me, creation—let no one put asunder!

This view of every stone pervaded by divinity seems to fit in well with Paul's vision of creation:

> *In Christ were created all things in heaven and on earth: everything visible and everything invisible.... Before anything was created, He existed, and He holds all things in unity* (Colossians 1:15-17 JB).

When you think about it, what holds reality together? Did God just wind up the universe like a clockmaker and walk away? Or does God spill into, hold together, and utterly transcend every atom and molecule of existence? *"The heaven and heaven of heavens cannot contain Him"* (2 Chron. 2:6).

Does God spill into, hold together, and utterly transcend every atom and molecule of existence?

This is another way of echoing what the Psalmist famously writes:

> *The heavens declare the glory of God,*
> *the vault of heaven proclaims His handiwork;*
> *day discourses of it to day,*
> *night to night hands on the knowledge* (Psalm 19:1-2 NJB).

> *Deep calls to deep in the roar of your waterfalls;*
> *all your waves and breakers have swept over me*
> (Psalm 42:7 NIV).

Nature can be a powerfully communicative touchstone of God in the Now, if we let it. Spending time in Creation can remove the human-time-bound veils over our eyes and awake us to the immediacy of what is.

You might consider going on a camp out, or a nature trail, and hear your heavenly Father speak afresh: *"Do I not fill heaven and earth?"* (Jer. 23:24 NIV). Nature itself speaks when we run out of words, as Jesus tells us (see Luke 19:40). And when our words and nature's words alike run out, a deafening truth echoes in the deep silence of the Now, as the intertestamental (between Old and New Testaments) apocrypha states:

> "We could say much more and still fall short; to put it concisely, 'He is all'" (Sirach 43:27 NJB).

All?

All—as we said earlier, it doesn't leave much out, does it? It's tempting, in our time-bound and fear-based default positions, to leave our most difficult and painful experiences outside the door of God's presence and care. And yet when we return to the Word, we get a glimpse of a God of both kindness and all-pervasiveness. Meditate on the following passages of Scripture and see what picture of God emerges:

> *Through Him all things came to be,*
> *not one thing had its being but through Him.*
> *All that came to be had life in Him*
> *and that life was the light of men,*
> *a light that shines in the dark,*
> *a light that darkness could not overpower* (John 1:3-5 JB).

For from Him and through Him and to Him are all things... (Romans 11:36 NIV).

One God and Father of all, who is over all and through all and in all (Ephesians 4:6 NIV).

...God is love. Whoever lives in love lives in God, and God in him (1 John 4:16 NIV).

And when everything is subjected to Him, then the Son Himself will be subject in turn to the One who subjected all things to Him, so that God may be all in all (1 Corinthians 15:28 JB).

Gods?

When you begin to see that all of reality is being birthed continuously by, through, and within God, sustained by God in every moment, unfolding from the Eternal Now, it really begins to mess with your head! You begin to see how our identities, hidden with Christ in God, are exalted in His grace, mercy, and adoption. You begin to see your own divinity emerge amidst God's All-ness.

This gets into admittedly dangerous territory. After all, wasn't lucifer's temptation to Adam and Eve in the Garden to think more of themselves than they ought—to be "as God" by eating of the fruit of the Tree of the Knowledge of Good and Evil? (See Genesis chapters 2 and 3 for this account.)

Yes, but that's not the whole story. In fact, it's not that they were thinking too highly of themselves at all, but rather that they thought too lowly of God. Judging Him to not want them to enjoy their God-given divinity in fellowship with Him in the Garden, they slandered His character. The serpent's lie was that Adam and Eve had to become god-like *without* God, whereas Abba's truth is that we grow into our God-like-ness in relating to Him as sons and daughters:

> *But to all who did accept Him He gave power to become children of God, to all who believe in the name of Him who was born not out of human stock or urge of the flesh or will of man but of God Himself* (John 1:12-13 JB).

We are forever creatures, but our relationship to our Creator is so close and intimate that it's difficult for the untrained eye to see where Christ ends and we begin:

> *"I am the vine, you are the branches"* (John 15:5a NKJV).

In Adam we lost sight of who we really are, but in Christ our eyes are being opened—we're beginning to see again:

> *Now this Lord is the Spirit, and where the Spirit of the Lord is, there is freedom. And we, with our unveiled faces reflecting like mirrors the brightness of the Lord, all grow brighter and brighter as we are turned into the image that we*

reflect; this is the work of the Lord who is Spirit (2 Corinthians 3:17-18 JB).

We're growing brighter and brighter as we approach each moment with wonder, savoring its unfolding. This is the life of dependence on God, who gives us each moment. In this way we apprentice ourselves to Jesus, and as Jesus promised, *"...fully trained* [students] *will be like their teacher"* (Luke 6:40b TNIV).

In this awakening to the Eternal Present, we are being trained for divinity. The apostle Peter gives us revelation in this regard:

> *For this is why the gospel was preached even to the dead, that though judged in the flesh like men, they might live in the spirit like God...* (1 Peter 4:6 RSV)

> [Christ] *has given us all the things that we need for life and for true devotion, bringing us to know God Himself...through them you will be able to share the divine nature* (2 Peter 1:3-4a JB).

This is why the early church father St. Maximus the Confessor encourages *divinity* as the proper and fitting aim for discipleship and sanctification:

> Let us become the image of the one whole God, bearing nothing earthly in ourselves, so that we may consort with God and become gods, receiving from God our existence as gods.[19]

Bold words? Absolutely! And they're echoed in much more recent times by C.S. Lewis in *The Weight of Glory*:

> It is a serious thing to live in a society of possible gods and goddesses, to remember that the dullest and most uninteresting person you talk to may one day be a creature which, if you saw it now, you would be strongly tempted to worship....[20]

 While we don't worship each other, we *do* revere the image of God in another.

While we don't worship each other, we *do* revere the image of God in another. If we began to love God *through* loving one another, we as a planet would be that much closer to fulfilling Jesus's great commandment. Jesus Himself reminded us of the awesome power and responsibility we bear as containers of the All in All:

> *Jesus answered: "Is it not written in your Law: I said, you are gods? So the Law uses the word gods of those to whom the word of God was addressed, and Scripture cannot be rejected"* (John 10:34-35 JB).

Jesus spoke this as a challenge to the Pharisees, that they not diminish their fellow countrymen, but live up to their high calling. We can take this as both encouragement and challenge as well. "The center of the soul is God," the 16th century Spanish mystic St. John of the Cross writes.[21] And his close friend and disciple St. Teresa of Ávila said, speaking of all of us, "Christ has no hands but yours."[22]

These realities go hand in hand with each other: We are joined to the Lord and are one spirit with Him, and those awakened to this reality become the hands and feet of Jesus in a world that feels, at the feeling and experience level, very far from God. If only they could see divine oneness and John 17 revelation! Well, the best argument for a creation in and through a God who's All in All is a people who are fully alive to this reality in the Eternal Now. Let's wake up together and show the world what they're missing out on!

Paul writes in Ephesians:

> *In this way we are all to come to unity in our faith and in our knowledge of the Son of God, until we become the perfect Man, fully mature with the fullness of Christ Himself* (Ephesians 4:13 JB).

Nothing less is at stake than the fully mature enjoyment and expression of Christ-consciousness on the Earth. Let's press in together.

God Is Everywhere and Never Nowhere

As you move deeper into this understanding—not just as an intellectual theory, but as a taste of the living

God—you will be bound to encounter misunderstanding from others. You might even wrestle with certain questions yourself—namely, what about all the suffering in the world? What about evil?

After all, if *everything* is a manifestation of God, this means that God is not only reflected in sunsets and moonbeams and nice people—God is also in the insane, infirm, and undesirable.

But is this any different than what Jesus told us? *"I tell you the truth, when you did it to one of the least of these My brothers and sisters, you were doing it to Me"* (Matt. 25:40 NLT). Or as Mother Teresa put it, "In the poor, we find Jesus in His most distressing disguises."[23]

To find God at home in the criminal and insane should not come as a shock. Does our own Scripture not (disturbingly) proclaim:

> *I form the light, and create darkness: I make peace, and create evil: I the* LORD *do all these things* (Isaiah 45:7).

Light and darkness, good and evil. God is not absent from any of life's circumstances. What our enemies plot for our harm, God transforms and means for good (see Gen. 50:20). And we know, from the overwhelming testimony of God's character in Scripture, as well as the ongoing testimony of God's work in our lives, that God is good, God is love, and God is bringing about the renewal of all things.

An All in All God doesn't shy away from the pain and bad stuff—God is just as immediate here as He is anywhere.

But an All in All God doesn't shy away from the pain and bad stuff—God is just as immediate here as He is anywhere.

And He's calling us to become participants in the divine nature by meeting Him in the least, last, and the lost—not shying away from the pain, but confronting it head on with the life of God.

We'll never know why so much evil happens this side of Heaven. But we can know where this Story is going; we know where this Uni-verse is headed: to greater and greater knowledge of the glory of the Lord. We can become living conduits of this glory by participating in the transfiguring of creation.

Hallelujah!

Questions to Ponder

It may be difficult to recognize where we think God is not. The Psalmist could not find a place to hide or run from God. Yet perhaps a revealing question to ask is: Where do you not want God to go? What places in your life do you wish to control by yourself? What things in your life seem to lack the presence of God?

_____

_____

_____

This chapter is infused with powerful statements. Which ones did you gloss over quickly because you agree with them? Which ones instigated disagreement in you? _____

_____

_____

Why? _____

_____

_____

_____

Living in the I AM
Exercise Seven: Letting God Be God

We are conditioned, particularly in Western culture, to experience God only in our tribe. In other words, in *my* religion, in *my* denomination, in *my* sub-sect, in my house of worship, with my small group, together with my clique of confidants. We have become so used to it that it seems normal, even routine. But if we are to let God be God and exist as bigger than us or our imaginations of Him, then we must be willing to release Him from our tribe.

The point of this exercise is to truly discover the vast richness of God that can be located wherever there are those seeking from an eager heart. It is also to cease discovering God for the purpose of "getting something." Isn't that often why we go to church? To get something? Perhaps why so many sacred assemblies feel dead is because countless numbers have been getting theirs and now little remains. These services simply need to be reinvigorated with the awareness of God's non-dual presence from a non-selfish heart.

Where Can't He Be Found Exercise

Go to two or three different churches, synagogues, mosques, or temples. Try to do it close together, such as on the same day. Make sure that one of them is an assembly that is familiar to you, perhaps a church that you were raised in. Next go to one completely different from your upbringing.

Something to note: It would be easy to condemn someone of another denomination, or especially another religion, as being irredeemably lost and worthy of nothing but condemnation or perhaps "witnessing." But it's far more challenging—and catalytic to growth—to apply your newfound understanding of God as All in All to see where He might be revealing traces of Himself in the other.

Remember that Jesus's bloodline includes many non-Jewish people and even prostitutes (see Matt. 1). A group of Bedouin magicians recognized the infant Jesus—when many of His own faith didn't—and presented Him with gifts. Jesus fellowshipped with heretical Samaritan women with no preconditions. As a follower of Jesus and one united with Him in the Spirit, you too can be an agent of God's scandalous grace and boundary-breaking discovery in the present moment. It is this with-ness that becomes the most radiant form of witness. Remaining rooted in both Spirit and Scripture will protect you (see John 16:13) from falsehood (which other denominations *as well as our own* can have; which other religions *as well as Christianity* contain).

Allow yourself to participate as much as you can, or that you find reasonable with your own conscience. Notice the ways you pull back or withhold yourself. See if, and how, you judge others as different. Attempt to open your heart to discovering the God to whom all truth belongs.

CHAPTER SEVEN

Awareness and Identification

To see a world in a grain of sand
And a Heaven in a wild flower,
Hold Infinity in the palm of your hand
And Eternity in an hour.
　　　—William Blake, "Auguries of Innocence"[1]

Consciousness itself does not hinder living in the present. In fact, it is only to a heightened awareness that the great door to the present opens at all.... Self-consciousness, however, does hinder the experience of the present.
　　　—Annie Dillard[2]

I am the light of the world.
—Jesus, John 8:12

You are the light of the world.
—Jesus, Matthew 5:14 NKJV

When listening to a symphony, you wouldn't tell the conductor to hold that note because you like it. The enjoyment of the symphony is in the revelation itself, progressing.
—Anthony De Mello[3]

"Know Thyself."
—inscription above the Oracle of Delphi[4]

We've spent a lot of time talking about who God is. But ironically, most of us spend all of our time thinking about ourselves. Not our higher selves, our true selves that are "hidden with Christ in God," but our smaller, more contingent selves—the surface-y stray thoughts, impulses, and emotions that we mistakenly over-identify with *who we are.* We are obsessed with this smaller self—thinking, feeding, entertaining, searching for a moment's happiness—the list is endless.

Overall, we are pre-occupied with this diminished sense of self. This is a very specific word choice; it implies inattentiveness because we are too crowded. Our attention has no space for anything else to enter. It is full of clutter! We cannot think about another person, and we cannot think about God. Our minds are pre-occu-pied with ourselves and the way we are going about our imaginary timelines. There is no room for the renewing of our minds.

Our culture exposes this pre-occupation all the time and plays to it—encouraging it to grow. "You deserve a break!" a billboard shouts with a picture of a giant cheeseburger behind it. There are commer-cials with women slowly licking spoons and clips of chocolate being poured ceaselessly while a voice sul-trily suggests, "Isn't it time you did something just for you?" Self "care" is all the rage when it comes to our cultural messaging.

Not only are our products marketed to our self-obsession, but entertainment as well. SimCity, a popular video game, has been a top-seller for several years. It boasts a program that allows you to develop your own virtual city and your own virtual life. There is strategy involved, but the game is about you—what you want to do. A similar game brings it down to you as a person: *Be* the character you wish you could be in real life. Cul-tivate a persona, choose a hobby, become the person of leisure you wish you could be. On and on we see the complete narcissism of this diminished-self focus. The film concept of cloning or creating avatars of ourselves has been (if you'll pardon the pun) replicated time and again by Hollywood. Clearly, we are pre-occupied with the surface of ourselves.

Sadly, this pre-occupation has nothing to do with being aware of ourselves or our surroundings. We can be completely out of touch with the present moment and equally removed from an accurate interpretation of ourselves. Earlier I mentioned how God saw Abram/Abraham—no longer an exalted father, but a father of many. It should be clear that *God's* vision of Abraham was what shaped him, not his own shifting self-thoughts. As Abraham abandoned himself to God's leading in the Eternal Now, his personhood became clear. As Abraham laid down his life, his life came more clearly into focus.

Our self pre-occupation is the biggest obstacle to living in the now.

If God created us, then it would make sense for us to want to know what He thinks about us—how He sees us. Please notice, our self pre-occupation is the biggest obstacle to living in the now. Awareness and identification are the keys to casting off this self-obsession. As we realize how self-centered we are, our awareness compels us to live into the light of God's present testimony concerning us.

What we don't realize is that God has made us for certain purposes—generally and specifically. God as Creator has given us names we need to inhabit. In Scripture, we find that the act of naming something describes its nature. The name, or the declaration, is meant to announce our nature. God formed us with personalities and capacities that we need to awaken to.

Notice that I say we need to awaken. We don't need to *become* something. What we don't understand is that we are "in" God right now. We are *already* something, in Christ's consciousness. Like the prophet Jonah, we cannot outrun God or hide from Him. Psalm 139 tells us of all the places we could go—the highest place or the lowest depths—and even there He would find us, and His right hand would hold us fast. We need to reposition ourselves to see ourselves as God does:

> ...*the Spirit and our spirit bear united witness that we are children of God. And if we are children we are heirs of God and coheirs with Christ, sharing His sufferings so as to share His glory* (Romans 8:16-17 NJB).

The first thing we can do to start seeing what God sees is to practice awareness. In other words, we need to pay attention to ourselves, our surroundings, and the present moment.

> Once the Buddha was asked, "Could you sum up your teaching on enlightenment [waking up] in one sentence?"
> He is said to have replied, "I can sum it up in one word!"
> "And what is that word?"
> "Awareness," replied the Buddha.

"Could you elaborate on that?" he was asked.
"Of course," replied the Buddha, "awareness is awareness is awareness."[5]

Remember, how we see ourselves is not necessarily true; it could be completely false.

Awareness is not so difficult. We can achieve awareness by simply observing ourselves. Much like SimCity, try paying attention to everything that you do, seeing it as if it were happening to someone else. In and of ourselves, we have a constant inner dialogue that is telling us who we are, what we should feel, and how we should react. We are rarely aware enough to hit the pause button to see if there is another opinion we should be listening to. Remember, how we see ourselves is not necessarily true; it could be completely false.

> "We usually fall, quite unawares, into assuming that what we are thinking—the ideas and opinions we harbor at any given time—are the 'truth' about what is 'out there' in the world and 'in here' in our minds. Most of the time, it just isn't so."
>
> —Jon Kabat-Zinn[6]

In order to grow into our God-given selves, we have to agree with God that we are who He says we are.

Watch yourself from the outside. This is the only way we can see ourselves without judgment, preconceptions, or comments. Let the noisy narrative die out.

As a human being, God gave you two eyes. This is what we use to see everything. However, in order to live in the Now, a different kind of sight is required of us. Some current-day teachers call this kind of sight the "third eye." I call it seeing with the mind of the Spirit. When we make the choice to move into the Now, we recognize that God has anointed our vision. Catholic teacher Richard Rohr says,

> No wonder all the great liturgical prayers of the churches end with the same phrase: "through Jesus Christ our LORD, Amen." We do not pray *to* Christ; we pray *through* Christ. Or even more precisely, Christ prays through us. We are always and forever the conduits, the instruments, the tuning forks, the receiver stations. (see Romans 8:22-27) The core task of all good spirituality is to teach us to "cooperate" with what God already wants us to do and has already begun to do. In fact, nothing good would even enter our minds unless in the previous moment God had not already "moved" within us. We are always and forever merely seconding the motion.[7]

A parable tells a story of three different men all watching the same sunset. The first man is happy to see the orange blush across the horizon and feel the air cool around him as the sun disappears. He is physically sensing the moment. The second man sees the orange strokes and is equally enjoying the moment. He is grateful for imagining the rotation of the Earth around the sun and the complex systems of astronomy. He senses the sunset physically as well as intellectually. The third man sees the same sunset, knowing and enjoying the same things that the first two men did; however, a silence settles into his being that the first two men did not have. He not only saw the sunset and could explain the reasons for the sunset, but he felt an awe for a greater mystery, coherence, and spaciousness that he could not articulate. This man was seeing with his third eye, which is to be the most insightful one.[8]

The third eye is seeing with the mind of the Spirit. It is not only sensory and factual, but mystical. It notices that there is something outside of ourselves that is separate from us and yet something we should be connected to: the I AM of God.

Paul summarizes it by reminding believers that the Spirit bears witness with us (see Rom. 8:14-17). This word *witness* is not an accident. God is "witnessing" us. He becomes the ultimate viewer. He is present to our minds, wills, and emotions. He cuts through the hard to discern regions of our hearts. Nothing is hidden from Him. As we are joined to Him, this witness is carried into us. God delivers His observation into our own understandings.

> The truly spiritual person does not have to be a witness to anything. A truly spiritual person is totally unselfconscious. A beautiful story illustrates this. "As I parked by the pond, I saw a lotus in full bloom. I instinctively said to her, 'How lovely you are, my dear, and how lovely must be the God who created you.' And she blushed because she had been quite unaware of her great beauty. And it gave her pleasure that God should be glorified. She was the lovelier for being so unselfconscious of her beauty, and she drew me because she made no attempt to catch my eye. Farther on was another pond where I found another lotus, spreading out her petals towards me and saying quite brazenly, 'Look at my beauty and give glory to my maker.' I walked away in disgust."[9]

Once more we draw on the apostle Paul, who informs us that the person who is joined to the Lord is made one spirit with Him (see 1 Cor 6:17). We have, through faith by becoming one with the Lord, access to God's awareness of our personhood. When we view ourselves through the mind of the Spirit, we see that all the things that God promised us, we already have. We are peace. We are love. We are forgiven. We are able to *identify* who we truly are.

Identification is the way in which we emotionally and mentally ground ourselves in something in or outside of us. I am rich. I am healthy.

Identification is the way in which we emotionally and mentally ground ourselves in something in or outside of us. I am rich. I am healthy. I am loved. Remember, *"as* [a man] *thinketh in his heart, so is he..."* (Prov. 23:7). Jesus knew who He was and where He came from. He didn't assume a personality or originate His purpose. He saw Himself exactly as He was— exactly as He is—by being one with the Father.

As John records it, Jesus prayed that His followers would be *in Him* just as He and the Father were one (see John 17). This is an insane kind of unity—an insane kind of identification. Think about it for just a minute: We get to identify with God, in God. And this is what Paul affirms later, *"But we have the mind of Christ"* (1 Cor. 2:16b NIV).

God sees you as a person of power. God sees you as self-sufficient—a person of power, accomplishment, potential, purpose, who has *all things*. You have everything you already need. If God sees you that way, then so be it. Think like God in that you see yourself through His eyes. He has given us everything we need for life and godliness (see 2 Pet. 1:3). We lack no good thing. God withholds no good thing from those whose walk is blameless (see Ps. 84:11)—timeless—in the present moment.

 No matter your age or stature, God sees you as self-sufficient and capable, as He has ordained you to be.

In the eternal I AM of God, you begin to realize that you have accomplished—you have arrived! No matter your age or stature, God sees you as self-sufficient and capable, as He has ordained you to be.

Seeing yourself the way that God sees you can be a difficult change of mind. The word *repent* means to "turn around" in Aramaic; "turn your mind around" and everything else will follow.

Jesus spent His entire life on Earth teaching people to change their minds around. When He spoke with the woman at the well, He was fully aware of the present moment, and He addressed her in her true identity.

Jesus explained to her that the time is coming, and has now come—the time *is* come—when His followers would worship in spirit and in truth. He was calling her mind to see the Eternal Present. He was inviting her to true life that He offers in Himself.

> This, I believe, is the path of awakening: the God who loved us before we were born, in whom we live and move and have our being, reaches out to us in the ways he knows will best awaken the seed that has been planted in us from eternity. As Paul told the philosophers on Mars Hill, God allots our times and places so that we "search for God and perhaps grope for him and find him—though indeed he is not far from each one of us" (see Acts 17:27).[10]

There are two types of thinking that exist within you. One is time-based, longing to live in the past and the future. It is busy with these thoughts. The other type of thinking gently questions itself: "Wait a minute! What about right now? What is going on right here in front of me?"

This questioning self is longing to identify with the I AM of God. The Christ who lives inside of you screams out, "I AM that I AM." And yet there is antichrist interference running here now, obscuring the truth of the Now. The root word meaning of *anti* means "instead of" not "against." So this *anti*christ static in our midst wants to be thinking on itself *instead of* Christ. It wants to keep us in time-based, distracted reality.

This *antichrist* static in our midst wants to be thinking on itself *instead of* Christ.

God says *"Behold, I am doing a new thing; now it springs forth, do you not perceive it?"* (Isa. 43:19a ESV). Christ is the Eternal Now. Can we work on the art of perception? Antichrist keeps us adrift in the past or future. Paul references this dual nature in Romans when he talks about the sin nature versus the redeemed self. "What I do, I don't want to do; and what I don't want to do, I do" (see Rom. 7).

Our minds exist, then, in a valley of decision. We must choose which way we are going to live. If we choose life, if we choose Christ as our hope, we have to cast off the antichrist mindset. We have to cast it off of us so that we are living in the freedom of awareness. In this sense, awareness becomes both the goal and the means to it. As we practice the art of awareness in the Spirit, we become aware of who we really are in Christ.

Questions to Ponder

What daily or weekly routine of yours, that you do for yourself, is your favorite? What takes the most time? For instance, do you work on your hair for an hour each morning? Do you take 30-minute showers or long baths? How long are your meal times? What things do you do for yourself that you enjoy? After identifying these things, ask yourself why they matter to you. What do these things reveal about your attitude toward yourself? _____

_____

_____

_____

Think back on the past few hours. Maybe the last few days or even weeks. Watch, in your mind's eyes, a video of your actions and words. As a neutral observer, what does this feel like? What things surprise you? Distress you? Make you proud of yourself? _____

_____

_____

_____

After you've watched your life video in your head, compare your thoughts or inner dialogue at the time to what you saw as an outsider. Are they congruent? Where is there conflict between your inner dialogue and your outward actions? _____

_____

_____

_____

Now, for a third time, watch your life video with God. Let Him join you in observing and ask Him what He sees. Do you agree with Him? What might He be saying to you about your true self? _____

_____

_____

_____

Living in the I AM
Exercise Eight: Contentment in Who You Are

Albert Camus, the noted existentialist philosopher said, "You will never be happy if you continue to search for what happiness consists of...."[11] It is so easy in today's culture to find happiness by proving who we are. Our identity, as we said earlier, is wrapped up in what we do, what we contribute to the world around us. The truth is, though, that everything we seek to prove through our sense of striving and doing is available to us here and now if we simply stop and pay attention. Why not stop the rat race—cease the endless cycle of defining identity through what you hold and have instead of who God has said you are.

Contentment Exercise 1

Today, stop several times, turn your focus to your breathing, relax as much as possible, then speak, "Lord Jesus"—slowly and with as little effort as possible. Perhaps it isn't more than a whisper. Breathe in, "Lord Jesus…." Breathe out, "Lord Jesus…." Then, notice the world around you and your place in it.

Contentment Exercise 2

Make a list of the things that God has said about you. What things has He declared of you? (Hint: Ephesians and Colossians contain fabulous truths of who we are in Christ. Try starting there.) For one day, every time you see the color green, practice "waking up" to who God has said you are.

CHAPTER EIGHT

Being Versus Having

It is a serious thing to live in a society of possible gods and goddesses, to remember that the dullest and most uninteresting person you talk to may one day be a creature which, if you saw it now, you would be strongly tempted to worship...

—C.S. Lewis[1]

Be holy, because I am holy.

—1 Peter 1:16 TNIV

Just to be is a blessing. Just to live is holy.

—Abraham Joshua Heschel[2]

Let us applaud and give thanks that we have become not only Christians but Christ himself. Do you understand, my brothers, the grace that God our head has given us? Be filled with wonder and joy—we have become veritable Christs!

—St. Augustine of Hippo[3]

The kingdom of God does not come with your careful observation [visibly], *nor will people say, "Here it is," or "There it is," because the kingdom of God is within you.*

—Jesus, Luke 17:20b-21 NIV

Look at the birds in the sky. They do not sow or reap or gather into barns; yet your heavenly Father feeds them. …And why worry about clothing? Think of the flowers growing in the fields; they never have to work or spin; yet I assure you that not even Solomon in all his regalia was robed like one of these.

—Matthew 6:26,28-29 JB

A Buddhist retreat master admitted to being a wealthy industrialist. He explains that ever since he started to practice silence and awareness, his business began to improve. Why? Because outside, he was working consistently, but inside of himself, he was relaxed and at rest. Whatever was happening, was happening through him as he let go. He wasn't doing it, he was letting it flow through him.[4] This is much like living in the Now and letting the eternal I AM live through you.

 The spirit realm doesn't care how much you know, and it doesn't care about your delineation of good versus bad—it cares about what life you have.

In the mind of humanity, there are two trees—the Tree of the Knowledge of Good and Evil and the Tree of Life. If we think about it, knowledge really can be good or bad. And when it comes to deciding what is what, we certainly get mixed up an awful lot. We call bad things good and good things bad all the time, relying on the limits of our own knowledge and understanding. The spirit realm doesn't care how much you know, and it doesn't care about your delineation of good versus bad—it cares about what life you have.

A lot of people eat from the wrong tree. They are bent on acquiring more information, developing their thoughts, and deciding what compartments these things conveniently fit into. This isn't the tree God invites us to eat from. In fact, this Tree of Knowledge produces the fruit of death. We were invited, by God, to eat from a different source. *Life* and *Now* go hand in hand. The truth is that the Now will bring you to Life.

God's Eternal Purpose grows on the vine of your life, hidden with Christ in God. It rests here, ever-ripe, waiting for you to take and eat. Will you stop eating the poison of knowledge long enough to taste and see the goodness of I AM?

As a human, you have eyesight and imagination. You are powerfully equipped to visualize reality. I once heard a well-known scientist and believer make the statement that what we don't know about the universe is less amazing than our capacity to know anything at all. Amazingly, we have been hardwired to see *something* of reality. Likewise, the eyes of our hearts can see the Now. Start seeing with your spirit, and believe it. Your belief system has to see the power of Now and the power of destiny and bring it into this moment.

Let's return to the Tree of the Knowledge of Good and Evil and the Tree of Life. These two trees exist in the spiritual sense as well. They represent the past and the Now. Scripture teaches us that knowledge puffs up. Often times we can take in information and knowledge and get full and fat on it—but this does nothing for us. This is not life. Yet the Tree of Life is what God said humanity could eat from. The Tree of Life represents the Now and freedom from the bondage of judgment that self-derived knowledge of good and evil inevitably creates. The Tree of Life represents the only form of truth. This is the Tree that God wants us to get our sustenance from.

One of the critical differences of these two trees and what they represent is that life really simply *is*. Like that bumper sticker says: "Life Happens!" There are not many qualifiers on life. What you see is what you get. It is what it is. That's why life really symbolizes living in the Now—and living in the Now draws us deeper into life. The Now is actually the fact of the matter, minus the judgments, the categorizing of something as good or bad, or even making sense of why it happened or where it's all going to end up.

Earlier I mentioned that the name of something reveals its nature. In the cultures of the Bible, this was especially true. Names depicted realities. This is one of the reasons why people symbolically changed their names. Abram becomes Abraham. Jacob becomes Israel. Saul becomes Paul. Often the disclosure of these names was considered so true that revealing them was an intimate affair. You didn't want just anybody knowing your core identity. To know that would mean that a person might have power over you—or so the thinking in those times went.

In light of this, it's interesting that Moses seemed driven to find out God's name. Many scholars believe this is an example of Moses attempting to gain control over God by having access to His personal name. Moses was after knowledge. He wanted to be able to understand God and to place Him in the appropriate box. God's answer is remarkable. He reveals that He simply is *I AM!*

The name of God is the ultimate affirmation in living in the Now and dwelling richly in life.

The disclosure is one that casts no judgments, draws no parallels, and guarantees no certainties. It denies our human ability to fulfill these categories. But instead of reducing God to a minimum, His I AM-ness provokes a radical freedom to be super-abundantly more than anything that we could have asked or imagined. The name of God is the ultimate affirmation in living in the Now and dwelling richly in life. It demonstrates that God is not interested in the fruit of the Tree of Knowledge of Good and Evil, with all of its judgments and cataloging of opinions. Instead God is interested in something far greater—*being*.

This has remarkable implications for daily living. Consider this the next time you're tempted to project or name your "future" plans. Don't say, "One day I *will* be a business owner." When you say "I will," you begin to search for the keys in the future to help you because you don't believe that you are sufficient enough now. But in reality, you *are* that businessman. You already are that person because God has made you for it. Your limited mind is telling you to keep that in the future, but it is simply not true. By isolating it to a future event, you're giving yourself license to not act on it immediately. You are able to drag your feet in the someday. You are living a half-life, being neither here nor there.

If you live in the power of the Now, you are able to walk confidently and deal with life as it is. You are able to speak things as they are—not as you wish them to be, not as you would rather imagine them, but as they are— as God sees them. If you live in the I AM of God, you live in the "I am rich, healthy, safe, prosperous"—not "I will," but "I have" and "I am." If you say "I will," you look for all the things that you need to do and gather to be it. But in reality, you already are everything that God says you are. The only difficulty is that you don't live in the I AM of being. When you do that, everything seems to line up with what you are thinking.

Incredibly, this business of eating the fruit of Life, of living in the Now, of existing in the I AM, is that everything in the universe seems to work for you. You aren't just already a shop owner—your life begins to unfold as if it already had been played out. It sounds crazy, but if you are thinking it, being it, and speaking it, the atmosphere is realigned to be in harmony with the commands of God. You are a child of God.

My favorite verse of Romans tells us, the God who *"calls things that are not as though they were"* (Rom. 4:17 NIV). In another version, it says God calls things that are not yet into being. The speaking of a thing as it is—the opening of our mouths—unleashes what God has already accomplished in our lives. Suddenly we are able to dwell richly in the super-abundance of God's Now-ness.

If you are thinking it, being it, and speaking it, the atmosphere is realigned to be in harmony with the commands of God.

If you begin to take the portion of the Lord's prayer that says, *"Give us this day our daily bread"* (Matt. 6:11) and you begin to believe that you *have* your daily bread, then you will start living daily with fresh revelation from God. You will be like the Israelites who lived upon the daily manna from Heaven. You will be living in the I AM of God.

I mentioned awareness in the previous chapter. Awareness is the thing that helps us to see in freedom, to see the Now as it truly is. How often are we focused on getting somewhere? The Now is not a stepping stone or a means to an end. No. We have to stop going places and getting things and start being places and having things. "Wherever you are, be all there."

He wants the weak to say, "I *am* strong" and the poor to say "I *am* rich." Just as Moses went before Pharaoh and said, "The I AM sent me," (see Exod. 7) so too we come before the circumstances restraining us from living into God's reality and we declare simply and unapologetically, "I am...!" Not I will be. Not one day or some day. But I am, today.

We are asked to *agree* with the truth of God. Whatever God is saying we are, we must agree with Him before blessing can flourish. And this requires great faith and courage. *"Do not let your hearts be troubled. Trust in God; trust also in Me"* (John 14:1 TNIV). God extends Himself to us as the intimate disclosure of the now and says, "Take, eat from this—the Tree of Life."

 Whatever God is saying we are, we must agree with Him before blessing can flourish.

Can we take a lesson from poets and tune our lives to I AM-bic pentameter?

Questions to Ponder

Which tree are you eating from? Quite simply, are you filling yourself with knowledge, or are you engaging yourself in life? _____

_____

_____

What are some dreams, goals, or longings of yours that are not yet met? What has prevented them from happening? How much responsibility do you bear for these things, and what is out of your control? _____

_____

_____

Do your dreams, goals, or longings match up or agree with what God says is true? If they are in agreement, what is stopping you from bringing life to them right now? _____

_____

_____

Like Ros Rinker's small prayer, what is the next step to these big dreams and hopes being realized? _____

_____

_____

_____

Living in the I AM
Exercise Nine: Finding God in Everything

If you've attempted any of the previous exercises, then you know how difficult contemplation is. Sitting and just being with the universe—as it is and not as we imagine it to be—allowing the sounds and the sensations to just wash over us and just being there with them. Noticing your awareness of comfort and discomfort, of this thought or that thought floating over you. It's been said that this practice of "awareness" is like a flashlight. You can train the spotlight on any object and just see it for what it is. Focusing the beam in different places shows you different things. Again, these are things you've probably noticed if you've integrated the activities into some form of daily routine.

Sometimes, however, we must become specifically mindful of elements that don't come naturally to our senses, namely the persistent presence of God. The point then of the following exercise is to continue the art of meditative awareness, but to also let our faculties be stimulated to recognize the invisible reality of God's being in everything.

Discovery of the Divine Exercise

Take your previous exercise in body awareness. Notice not just the sensations, but also the grosser and more subtle realities and sensations. Indigestion. Queasiness. Numbness. Cold. Just allow yourself to feel those sensations. Try to do the same with the sounds that you are aware of. Notice as many as you can, but be careful not to label them as you take note.

As you do this, you will probably become aware of a peace, a tranquility, in your spirit. If this happens to you, just relax into it. Let the here and now feel good. Now, express these sensations to God, but do so without words. Try pretending that you can only speak to God with your face and your eyes and your hands and your breath. Tell God that it is so good to find Him here, everywhere, even in unpleasant experiences.

Now, return to the world of awareness. Become mindful of the air you are breathing, the sounds surrounding you, the sensations of your body. Claim these things as the experience of God in this moment. Even audibly whisper to God, "Lord, *this* is You!" Become open to the whole world around you—become open to God.

CHAPTER NINE

Taking Risk

I'm in the market for some present tense. It's a seller's market—do you think I won't sell all that I have to buy it?

—Annie Dillard[1]

God is love. Whoever lives in love lives in God, and God in him.

—1 John 4:16 NIV

I tell you most solemnly, whoever believes in Me will perform the same works as I do Myself; he will perform even greater works.

—Jesus, John 14:12 JB

Be realistic. Plan for a miracle.
—Bhagwan Shree Rajneesh[2]

Behold, I am with you always, to the end of the age.
—Jesus, Matthew 28:20 ESV

[God] *said that we were "gods" and He is going to make good His words. If we let Him—for we can prevent Him if we choose—He will make the feeblest and filthiest of us into a god or goddess, dazzling, radiant, immortal creature, pulsating all through with such energy and joy and wisdom and love as we cannot now imagine, a bright stainless mirror which reflects back to God perfectly (though, of course, on a smaller scale) His own boundless power and delight and goodness. The process will be long and in parts very painful; but that is what we are in for.*
—C.S. Lewis[3]

The sea may be as still as glass or as white and angry as it is against the Cliffs of Moher in Ireland. Either way, stepping onto the water and expecting to stay afloat is impossible. Abandoning the past and future and having faith for the Now may sound a little bit like asking you to walk on water. It is truly depending on the miraculous. May I remind you, friend, that none of it is impossible to God. The Eternal I AM is your Father, your Maker, your Sustainer, and your Teacher.

If He asks you to follow Him where He's going, then there is no better direction to take. Planning for the miracle is then an action of true realism—but it does demand a solitary act of taking a risk.

 Planning for the miracle is then an action of true realism—but it does demand a solitary act of taking a risk.

Taking risks for the Kingdom and being willing to live in the Now is not easy.

But as Peter and James and John were called to be fishers of men, you are called to cast your nets and your thought patterns into the Now. It sounds risky and rare, but God is asking you to do it. Who better could you listen to? The disciples couldn't think of anyone else to trust. *"Lord, to whom shall we go? You have the words of eternal life"* (John 6:68 NIV).

When you change your mind, you will see how it is in the Now. Step off the boat like Peter did when Jesus said, *"Come"* (Matt. 14:29 NIV). Take your mind out of the boat, the comfort zone that leaves you handicapped. The waters have no foundation in reality. They are representative of "faith." And behold, Jesus was an ever-present help in a time of trouble (see Ps. 46:1). He kept Peter afloat with His loving-kindness and His steady hand. And He will lift you to where you should be.

The Canaanite woman believed for healing (see Matt. 15:21-28). She needed just one word to heal her daughter's illness. She reached into the future through faith. Just like the God we believe in that calls things that are not as though they were, she reached into the promise and brought it into the power of the Now. She received a Jewish healing even though she was a Canaanite. What did Christ honor? Her belief was fully dependent on His follow-through. He honored her obedience to living in the Now and believing in the Eternal I AM of God. He also honored that obedience in the face of oppression and risk. Calling the promises of God into the Now may cost us something. It makes a demand upon us.

Once again, like always, Paul has something to teach us about this. You've heard the expression "count the cost." This is what Paul asks us to do. Consider carefully who and what you are following. For Paul, the decision had a clear ending. He considered his life worth *nothing* to him if only he could be found *in* Christ. All Paul desired was to be living in the I AM of God, moving in the power of the present (see Phil. 3).

Sometimes stepping out in faith also means laying down our lives as living sacrifices to be consumed by the Fire of God.

Quite honestly, taking risk to step into the Now of God means accepting the possibility of getting hurt. While we believe and can know with certainty that God cares for those He loves, we also know that God's ways are really not our own. Sometimes stepping out in faith also means laying down our lives as living sacrifices to be consumed by the Fire of God. I've never known a fire that didn't burn up everything in its path. The risk of living in the Now is also one of being singed, even burned. However, if we are to know God as He is, then the danger is acceptable. Together with Paul we *"consider that our present sufferings are not worth comparing with the glory that will be revealed in us"* (Rom. 8:18 NIV).

This is so difficult and admittedly requires practice. Think of a trapeze artist whose great feats of aerial acrobatics amaze us. They take leaps and hurdles that seem incalculable and full of risk. How are they able to get over their fear? I think it's quite simple: They didn't start with the big jumps first. They practiced. They put in the time to practice. They committed themselves to a thousand tiny leaps—simply the ones they had to undertake in the moment. Similarly we are invited to engage today—nothing more. God has promised us that we have strength for the day. He has not spoken much about tomorrow, except to say that it is worthless to worry about it, that His compassions fail not, and that His mercies are new every morning (see Lam. 3:23; Matt. 6:34).

Taking a risk means accepting that Now is just the place God has fashioned for us. He has not given us something out of our league. He hasn't saddled us with something that we'll only have the strength to deal with some time in the future. Let tomorrow take care of itself! Today is what we've been given to live within, along with the capacity to encounter it.

In a way this type of knowledge both accepts risk and the possible dangers that come along with it, but also believes that God is capable of making a way in the face of such adversity. As one famous evangelist responded when a heckler in the crowd asked how he dealt with the problem of pain and disease in this life, "Our God Heals!" This is beautiful, and it is also the message of the cross and the resurrection. There is no darkness incapable of being brought into glorious light. There is no evil outside of being redeemed. This demolishes our fear of tomorrow, doesn't it? Indeed, we can anticipate God's best no matter how bleak the immediate prognosis.

The River of God

I went hiking today and ended up sweating for eight miles. Fortunately for me, the trail followed a rushing creek that gave me several good ideas. I got down to the water's edge and stuck my hand in to check the temperature—icy cold. For the entire hike, I heard the roar of the water, and now I watched the clear waters slip past me faster than I could notice. It reminded me that we never step into the river twice and feel the same thing. The same water will never touch us, no matter how much we jump and skitter.

God is an ever-flowing river. There is always something new, fresh, alive, and revelatory with Him. There is a freshness within His presence. If you step outside of Him, things are dry and dull. In I AM, life is fresh and alive. This means that the fear of failure created by problems in the past is negated in the newness of Now. We can accept God's new mercies, today.

 God is an ever-flowing river. There is always something new, fresh, alive, and revelatory with Him.

The "Lot" Within

When Abraham and Lot traveled together, God told Abraham that unless they separated, God would not show Abraham the full promise. Lot was like the "veil" that needed to be removed. For Abraham, it was likely easier to travel with his nephew—safety in numbers, camaraderie. Yet God asked him to take Him up on a risk, to have faith.

The "Lot" in our lives says to us, "We'll get there. It's going to happen. Just stick with me for a while." But

Lot lies to you. The hope of comfort now and maybe greatness later is not to be trusted. Like Abraham, we need to separate from the "Lots" that (or who) are telling us to settle for the safety of our present way of life. Every moment we wait is a moment we waste. It is also a moment we cease walking in faith. To wait means to *bind* or *twist together*. This is exactly what happens when we hesitate to act on what God is calling us toward. We ended up getting twisted up with our "Lot" and start drifting away from a risky offering.

The disciples were great examples of risk takers always counting the cost and hoping to hold onto something they could understand. They hoped to always be with Jesus and to understand what He talked about. He spoke of future glory, and James and John envisioned the accolades of Heaven for themselves. Even while spending physical time with the living God, the disciples still couldn't be fully present with Him. They were hoping for the future.

When Jesus first called His group of friends, He sought them out in their places of work—the seaside, their boats, the city streets. Matthew records it simply and clearly for us in chapter 4:

> *As Jesus was walking beside the Sea of Galilee, He saw two brothers, Simon called Peter and his brother Andrew. They were casting a net into the lake, for they were fishermen. "Come, follow Me," Jesus said, "and I will make you fishers of men."*

*At once they left their nets and followed Him.
Going on from there, He saw two other brothers, James son of Zebedee and his brother John.
They were in a boat with their father Zebedee,
preparing their nets. Jesus called them, and
immediately they left the boat and their father
and followed Him* (Matthew 4:18-22 NIV).

For three years, Jesus spoke to them about the Kingdom. He described how to live fully, to do what is in
front of them, to abide in Him and with Him. He was
teaching them how to live in the I AM of God. Yet they
didn't quite get it. After Jesus was killed, they laid Him
in a tomb and went back to their homes in mourning.
What was that second day like? Did the disciples have
much to say, or did they just suffer through the silence?

The female disciples took a risk in going to the
tomb that Sunday morning. Who knows what was in
their hearts that day? But they brought oil and spices
to anoint the body of their Rabbi. Their hearts may
not have risked believing in a resurrection, but they
did show courage and love by going out to the tomb
of a man who had been so dramatically crucified two
days earlier.

Remember that Jesus's death was no small matter
that took place in a quiet room or a back alley. During
Jesus's trial and death sentence, the disciples fled. Peter
was afraid to tell a servant girl he was an actual disciple. Not one of the 12 were present or made themselves

available to help Jesus carry His cross. The risk in standing with their Rabbi was too frightening for them.

Jesus was not even buried by His best friends! They were still absent. According to John, Joseph of Arimathea and Nicodemus, the man who went to meet Jesus in the night to ask about salvation—they requested permission to bury the body. They got the tomb and wrapped the body themselves. The 12 disciples were gone, and Jesus's secret followers finally stepped meekly forward to bury the man they had hoped to believe in. Yet the women decided it was worth the risk of ridicule or rejection to go to the tomb and mourn properly.

Fortunately, they were not met by men or a corpse, but angels! When they ran back to tell the other disciples, Luke records that the disciples *"did not believe the women, because their words seemed to them like nonsense"* (Luke 24:11 NIV). But Peter ran to the tomb to see for himself.

The disciples gathered back in their locked room that day, according to John. John recorded that the doors of the house they were staying were locked, yet Jesus showed up in their midst (see John 20:19). Mourning at home with the doors locked for fear of the Jews does not sound like taking a risk, does it? Rather it seems like they avoided every risk possible.

Sometime later, during the 40 days that Jesus stirred up His old stomping grounds, He surprises the disciples again. Peter had decided to go fishing. Whether they needed fish or he thought it was a recreational activity, we don't know. But we do know that that was Peter's job before he met Jesus. Though Jesus had resurrected Himself, proven Himself alive, and told His disciples to continue to teach others of the Kingdom, here is Peter, again, shoving off to sea, fishing for fish and not for people (see John 21). He is putting his hands to the nets rather than to the people. He is looking down for a comforting catch rather than looking out and giving life. He is back in the boat.

When Peter recognizes Jesus fully, he jumps into the water, apparently hoping to get to Jesus in a more dramatic fashion. Perhaps he just couldn't wait patiently for rowing to bring him into shore. Once reunited, Jesus feeds them baked fish. Poignantly, symbolically, Jesus asks Peter if he loves Him.

> *When they had finished eating, Jesus said to Simon Peter, "Simon son of John, do you truly love Me more than these?"*
> *"Yes, Lord," he said, "You know that I love You."*
> *Jesus said, "Feed My lambs."*
> *Again Jesus said, "Simon son of John, do you truly love Me?"*
> *He answered, "Yes, Lord, You know that I love You."*
> *Jesus said, "Take care of My sheep."*
> *The third time He said to him, "Simon son of John, do you love Me?"*

Peter was hurt because Jesus asked him the third time, "Do you love Me?" He said, "Lord, You know all things; You know that I love You."

Jesus said, "Feed My sheep" (John 21:15-17 NIV).

It is as if each question is meant to negate Peter's three denials. Jesus gives him three chances to redeem his cowardice. Though Peter did not take risk before, Jesus patiently offers another opportunity. Jesus brings it down to the simplest language for Peter now. "Feed My sheep. Take care of My sheep. Follow Me." It is that simple.

As long as we maintain a tight-fisted grip on how we think a situation should go, we cease to allow for God's unpredictable best.

Saying "yes" to God actually means something very significant. It translates into surrendering control. As long as we maintain a tight-fisted grip on how we think a situation should go, projecting our idea of what would be "better," we cease to allow for God's unpredictable best. We are like Peter, going back to our boats, gathering our nets to ourselves.

Abraham had no clue that leaving the familiarity of Lot would release such a glorious outcome. It must have seemed tragic and out of his control. Still, he was willing to open his hands and surrender to God. This is the nature of risk taking. It releases the cares of the moment into the all-inviting hands of the source of the Now. The risk is in our letting go; yet I AM's hands are the surest place to trust ourselves into. We risk stepping our feet in front of us, into the Now, yet He watches patiently and full of love, making our footing firm.

As with Peter, so it is with us. Keep walking, friends. Let go of your "Lots" for God's *all*.

Questions to Ponder

What are your greatest fears of living in the freedom that you desire and that God offers? _____

_____

_____

What might you lose in order to live in the I AM of God? _____

_____

_____

Like a musician in training, or the trapeze artist fly-ing through the air, how can you practice taking risk? What steps can build your faith and your joy in living in the Now? _____

_____

_____

_____

Are you holding onto a "Lot"? How does this make you feel secure? What promises of God can you find or remember that encourage you to let "Lot" go? What future promise may He be offering you? _____

_____

_____

_____

_____

Living in the I AM
Exercise Ten: Risking

Part of our deep inability to take a leap of faith is actually wrapped up in another wonderful virtue: hope. Now, hope is actually an intense longing for that which we cannot or do not yet see; it is an intense wresting of the future into the present. Hope is an active thing. However, hope is often distorted into a sort of drug, lulling us into inaction. By relegating the possible good to the future, pining and wishing for one day and some day, we give ourselves wide latitude for pure passivity.

In truth "the hard times" aren't coming to an end any time soon. Life in the present is a struggle. That's not changing. It's time to stop waiting for what you desire. Accept what is and take hold of what is to come. Don't wait anymore. Don't buy into the illusion that a future moment will resolve your problems.

Stop waiting. Do what you love. Do what you are called to do. Do what you wish you could if only…. Take the first steps right now.

Risk Exercise

Spend one hour a day doing what you sense in your spirit that you must do—regardless of your daily constraints. This may take the form of painting or running or starting a business or selling everything you have and being a missionary in Zimbabwe. It could also be something more internal, like being mindful of your heart attitude and praying a simple prayer. It could even be simply calling your mother or father and speaking to them.

Most often this takes the form of taking steps in the present toward realizing the things you've always dreamed about doing if you only had more time or greater resources. Start now. Do what you can. But let me warn you, you may discover that you cannot or do not wish to actually go down the path you thought you did. Unrealized dreams allow us to imagine ourselves as different from what we often are, and when we aggressively take steps toward their consummation, we are occasionally in for a rude awakening. That's alright. Take it for what it is and move forward.

CONCLUSION:

Forward to Now

One day a disciple searching for enlightenment ended his journey by coming at last to the most learned guru in all the world. He wore the appropriate sannyasi robes and appeared to have freshly shaved his head, showing penitence and devotion. He knew the proper words and all the formal ways of demonstrating respect for a Master. The guru asked him why he had come to see him and the man replied, "For many years I have been searching for God and enlightenment. I have looked everywhere that God is supposed to be: in churches and temples, on mountain tops, in the wilderness, the solitude of monasteries; I have even given everything I had to the poor, and I have even lived among the lepers, tending to them as they died."

"And have you found God? Have you been enlightened?" asked the guru.

"No. No I have not. You are surely enlightened, oh wise one. Tell me, have you found God?"

The Master stood quietly. What could he say to this question? As the evening sun cast its last golden hues upon the ground a thousand sparrows stirred in a nearby grove of trees. Off in the distance there was the bustle of traffic and human activity. A bullfrog groaned out his call for love. The mosquitoes hummed little warnings that they would soon attack. All around life was pulsing and stirring. And still, this seeker could ask about finding God.

At last the Master said, "God is Now."

The disciple sat for a long time wondering about this. After a good while, he went away, disappointed and began to search someplace else.

God is radically available as we abide in the here and now.

The secret—in our search for God and in our quest for both intimacy with Him and peace in the present moment— is that *there is no secret*. God is radically available as we abide in the here and now. The words of the wise Master ring true and echo with the eternal voice of disclosure first made known to Moses;

God's true name is Yahweh, "I AM." God is Now. Look around you. Listen with your ears. Feel with your skin. Allow the events this very instant to cascade around you. It is in this way that we practice God's presence.

Both Old and New Testaments disclose a God who is not only situated in the present moment, in the Now, but actually is the fullness of that reality. Through the stories of Abraham, Isaac, and Jacob, we begin to catch a glimmer of God's relationship to people who would live into the Now. We are asked to strike out, to take a daring leap, to literally leave the land of the past and advance into the here and now.

This is certainly a risk. But as we lean toward our divine purpose we find that it is no risk at all; we are installing ourselves in the all-consuming and all-pervading presence of God. Moreover, we are invited into a deeper awareness, which isn't to say some sort of narcissistic self-absorption, but rather an identification with the Light of God's present calling in our lives. The biblical accounts are riddled with illustration after illustration of discovering God as All and Only in relationship to the Now.

Jesus's often cryptic statements, such as, *"…Where I am, you cannot come"* (John 7:34 NIV) or *"…Before Abraham was, I am"* (John 8:58), stand as powerful reminders that the Incarnate Son exists in relationship to God's I AM-ness, His "nowness" of being. Jesus isn't caught in a deadpan relationship with the past. He isn't pining away for the future. Instead He has said, *"Let the dead bury their dead…"* (Matt. 8:22) and that not even He *"knows about that day or hour…"* (Matt. 24:36 NIV). These indicate that He isn't invested in trying to come up with an insurance policy for tomorrow. Jesus is in the same business that His Father is, that Yahweh, the I AM, is. What's even more incredible is that we too are asked to join in the eternal occupation of dwelling in the present moment.

We get our past and future back, but as gifts to be cherished rather than tyrants that torment us.

As we begin to relax in the now, a wonderful thing happens: We get our past and future back, but as gifts to be cherished rather than tyrants that torment us. The people of God from ancient Israel tell and re-tell stories of God's wonderful past works; we have glorious future hopes to anticipate. We are a storied people; we are a hope-filled people. But past and future close in on us like a vise if we do not recognize God in the only place we actually have: the Now. From Now, past and future sparkle and inspire. From Now, we are given the anointing, the "eye salve" that allows us to see the grand march of time for the divine symphony it is.

God is calling a today people to partner with Him in the precious present moment. Are you ready? If so, be alive—stay curious—wake up!

Endnotes

Chapter One

1. Meister Eckhart, *Meister Eckhart's Sermons* (New York: Cosimo Inc., 1909, 2007), 19.

2. Jean Pierre De Caussade, *Abandonment to Divine Providence* (New York: Cosimo Inc., 1921, 2010), 40.

3. Osho, *Awareness: The Key to Living in Balance* (New York: St. Martin's, 2001), 51.

4. Anthony de Mello, *Song of the Bird* (New York: Image, 1982).

5. A summary paraphrase of Madam Jean Guyon, *Experiencing the Depths of Jesus Christ,* 3rd edition (Christian Books Publishing House, 1981).

Chapter Two

1. Brother Lawrence quote: http://www.iwise.com/bLYTW (accessed December 4, 2010).

2. Frank Laubach, quoted in "In Others' Words: On Practicing God's Presence"; http://www.practicegodspresence.com/reflections/others_words.html (accessed December 4, 2010).

3. Jean Pierre De Caussade, *Abandonment to Divine Providence* (New York: Cosimo Inc., 1921, 2010), 70.

4. Ancient folk tale, as told in Anthony de Mello, *The Song of the Bird* (New York: Image, 1982).

Chapter Three

1. Eckhart Tolle, *The Power of Now: A Guide to Spiritual Enlightenment* (Vancouver, BC: Namaste Publishing, 1999), 48.

2. Anthony de Mello, *The Way to Love: The Last Meditations of Anthony de Mello* (New York: Image Books, Doubleday, 1995).

3. Brother Lawrence, *The Practice of the Presence of God With Spiritual Maxims* (Grand Rapids, MI: Spire Books, Baker Publishing, 1958, 2006).

4. Groundhog Day movie, Directed by Harold Ramis (Sony Pictures, 1993, 2001), DVD.

5. Belinda Carlisle, "Heaven Is a Place on Earth," *Heaven on Earth* (MCA, 1990).

Chapter Four

1. Frank Laubach, quoted in "In Others' Words: On Practicing God's Presence"; http://www.practicegodspresence.com/reflections/others_words.html (accessed December 4, 2010).

2. Brother Lawrence, quoted in Ibid.

3. Rosalind Rinker, *Prayer: Conversing With God* (Grand Rapids, MI: Zondervan, 1986).

4. Anthony de Mello, *Sadhana, A Way to God: Christian Exercises in Eastern Form* (New York: Image, 1984), 16.

Chapter Five

1. Annie Dillard, *Pilgrim at Tinker Creek* (New York: Bantam, Harper Collins, 1974).

2. Eckhart Tolle, *Stillness Speaks* (Vancouver, BC: Namaste Publishing, 2003).

3. J. Francis Stroud, *Praying Naked.* (New York: Image Books, 2005).

4. Thomas Aquinas—"We remain joined to Him as one unknown"—as quoted in Sam Keen interview; http://www.scottlondon.com/interviews/keen.html (accessed December 4, 2010).

Chapter Six

1. St. Basil the Great, *Adversus Eunomium 4.*

2. St. Thomas Aquinas, *The Catechism of the Catholic Church,* Opusc. 57:1-4.

3. St. Irenaeus, *Adv Haer III,* 19,1.

4. Contra Gentes and De Incarnatione, ed./trans. Robert W. Thomson (Oxford: Oxford University Press, 1971).

5. C.S. Lewis, *The Grand Miracle* (New York: Ballantine Books, 1986), 85.

6. Wayne Dyer, *You'll See It When You Believe It* (New York: Harper Collins, 2001), 2.

7. J.B. Phillips, *Your God Is Too Small* (New York: Touchstone, Simon & Schuster, 1952, 1997).

8. Brother Lawrence, *The Practice of the Presence of God with Spiritual Maxims* (Grand Rapids, MI: Spire Books, Baker Publishing, 2006).

9. Jean Pierre De Caussade, *The Sacrament of the Present Moment* (New York: Harper Collins, 1989).

10. Tommy Tenney, *God Chasers* (Shippensburg, PA: Destiny Image Publishers, 2005).

11. Eckhart Tolle, The *Power of Now: A Guide to Spiritual Enlightenment* (Vancouver, BC: Namaste Publishing, 1999, 2010).

12. Rhonda Byrne, *The Secret* (New York: Atria Books, 2006).

13. Rabbi Baal Shem Tov and Rabbi Sfat Emet, quoted in Jay Michaelson, *Everything is God: The Radical Path of Nondual Judaism* (Boston: Trumpeter Books, 2009), 27.

14. Original translation by Jay Michaelson, *Everything Is God.*

15. Michaelson, 27.

16. Ibid.

17. Ken Wilbur, *A Brief History of Everything* (Boston: Shambala Publications, 1996), 27.

18. Moses Cordovero, quoted in Michaelson.

19. St. Maximus the Confessor, "Various Texts on Theology, the Divine Economy, and Virtue and Vice" Howell Palmer, Sherrard, and Ware, *The Philokalia* (London: Faber and Faber Limited, 1981), 171.

20. C.S. Lewis, *The Weight of Glory* (New York: HarperOne, 2001).

21. St. John of the Cross, *The Living Flame of Love by St. John of the Cross With His Letters, Poems, and Minor Writings,* trans. David Lewis (New York: Cosimo Classics, 1912, 2007).

22. St Teresa of Avila, quoted in Elizabeth Andrew, *On the Threshold* (Cambridge: Westview, 2005).

23. Mother Teresa. *Where There is Love, There is God: A Path to Closer Union with God* (New York: DoubleDay, 2010), 53.

24. C.S. Lewis, "The Grand Miracle," *God on the Dock: Essays on Theology and Ethics,* ed. Walter Hooper (Grand Rapids, MI: Eerdmans Publishing, 1970, 2001), 80-89.

Chapter Seven

1. William Blake, "Auguries of Innocence," *The Complete Poetry & Prose of William Blake* (New York: Anchor, 1997).

2. Annie Dillard, *Pilgrim at Tinker Creek* (New York: Bantam, Harper Collins, 1974), 82.

3. Anthony de Mello, quoted in Francis J. Stroud, *Praying Naked: The Spirituality of Anthony de Mello* (New York: Image Books, Double Day, 2005).

4. Richard Rohr, *The Naked Now: Learning to See as the Mystics See* (New York: Crossroad Publishing, 2009).

5. Stroud, 219.

6. Jon Kabat-Zinn, *Wherever You Go, There You Are* (New York: Hyperion, 1994), xiv.

7. Rohr, 23.

8. *Ibid.*

9. Stroud, 219.

10. Leighton Ford, *The Attentive Life: Discerning God's Presence in All Things* (Downers Grove, IL: Intervarsity Press, 2008), 75.

11. Albert Camus, *Youthful Writings* (Vintage Books, 1977).

Chapter Eight

1. C.S. Lewis, *The Weight of Glory* (New York: Harper Collins, 1949, 2001).

2.

3.

4. Anthony de Mello, *Song of the Bird* (New York: Image, 1982).

Chapter Nine

1. Annie Dillard, *Pilgrim at Tinker Creek* (New York: Bantam, Harper Collins, 1974), 86.

2. Bhagwan Shree Rajneesh, as quoted in *Ancient Music in the Pines* (Osho Media International).

3. C.S. Lewis, *Mere Christianity* (New York: Harper Collins, 1952, 2001), 174-175.

JOURNAL

_____
_____
_____
_____
_____
_____
_____
_____
_____
_____
_____
_____
_____
_____
_____
_____
_____
_____
_____
_____
_____
_____
_____

JOURNAL

JOURNAL

Journal

JOURNAL

JOURNAL

JOURNAL

JOURNAL

JOURNAL

Journal

JOURNAL

JOURNAL

Journal

JOURNAL

JOURNAL

_____

_____

_____

_____

_____

_____

_____

_____

_____

_____

_____

_____

_____

_____

_____

_____

_____

_____

_____

_____

_____

_____

JOURNAL

JOURNAL

About Jeremy Lopez

Dr. Jeremy Lopez is Founder and President of Identity Network International (www.identitynetwork.net), an apostolic and prophetic resource website that reaches well over 150,000 people around the globe, distributing books and audio teachings on the prophetic move of God. Jeremy has prophesied to thousands of people from all walks of life, including congregations, producers, investors, business owners, attorneys, city leaders, musicians, and various ministries around the world concerning areas such as finding missing children, financial breakthroughs, parenthood, and life-changing decisions.

Dr. Jeremy Lopez is an international teacher and motivational speaker, speaking on new dimensions of revelatory knowledge in Scripture, universal laws, mysteries, patterns, and cycles. His life and ministry are marked by a love for all people and desire to enrich their lives with love, grace, and the mercy of God. He believes this is the hour for the sons of God to arise. This ministry desires to see every believer awake to their destiny. Dr. Jeremy believes it is time to awaken to the fullness of our God-given divine consciousness and live a life filled with potential, purpose, and destiny.

Dr. Jeremy teaches the principle that we are positioned in heavenly places and are called to minister out of that realm. He shares this vision in conferences, prophetic meetings, and church services. He serves on many governing boards, speaks to business leaders across the nation, and holds a Doctorate of Divinity. He has ministered in many nations including Jamaica, Indonesia, Haiti, Hong Kong, Taipei UK, Mexico, Singapore, and the Bahamas. He has hosted and been a guest on radio programs from Indonesia to New York.

He is the author of *The Power of the Prophetic Spirit* and *The Three Dimensions of Finances* and has recorded over 40 audio teachings. Jeremy's ministry has been recognized by many other prophetic leaders around the nation.

You can go to Jeremy's website for more resources and sign up for his E-mail newsletters and prophetic words at:

www.identitynetwork.net

You may contact us by E-mail at:

Customerservice@identitynetwork.net

IN THE RIGHT HANDS, THIS BOOK WILL CHANGE LIVES!

Most of the people who need this message will not be looking for this book. To change their lives, you need to put a copy of this book in their hands.

> *But others (seeds) fell into good ground, and brought forth fruit, some a hundred-fold, some sixty-fold, some thirty-fold* (Matthew 13:8).

Our ministry is constantly seeking methods to find the good ground, the people who need this anointed message to change their lives. Will you help us reach these people?

> *Remember this—a farmer who plants only a few seeds will get a small crop. But the one who plants generously will get a generous crop* (2 Corinthians 9:6).

EXTEND THIS MINISTRY BY SOWING
3 BOOKS, 5 BOOKS, 10 BOOKS, OR MORE TODAY,
AND BECOME A LIFE CHANGER!

Thank you,

Don Nori Sr., Publisher
Destiny Image
Since 1982

DESTINY IMAGE PUBLISHERS, INC.

*"Speaking to the Purposes of God for This Generation
and for the Generations to Come."*

VISIT OUR NEW SITE HOME AT
WWW.DESTINYIMAGE.COM

FREE SUBSCRIPTION TO DI NEWSLETTER

Receive free unpublished articles by top DI authors, exclusive

discounts, and free downloads from our best and newest books.

Visit www.destinyimage.com to subscribe.

Write to: Destiny Image
              P.O. Box 310
              Shippensburg, PA 17257-0310

Call: 1-800-722-6774

Email: orders@destinyimage.com

For a complete list of our titles or to place an order
online, visit www.destinyimage.com.

FIND US ON FACEBOOK OR FOLLOW US ON TWITTER.

www.facebook.com/destinyimage   facebook
www.twitter.com/destinyimage   twitter